AuthorTalk

Author Talk

compiled
and
edited by
Leonard S.
Marcus

conversations with

JUDY BLUME
BRUCE BROOKS
KAREN CUSHMAN
RUSSELL FREEDMAN
LEE BENNETT HOPKINS
JAMES HOWE
JOHANNA HURWITZ
E. L. KONIGSBURG
LOIS LOWRY
ANN M. MARTIN
NICHOLASA MOHR
GARY PAULSEN
JON SCIESZKA
SEYMOUR SIMON
and
LAURENCE YEP

✳

Simon & Schuster Books for Young Readers

NEW YORK   LONDON   TORONTO   SYDNEY   SINGAPORE

For Gary,
who asks good questions
—L. M.

Simon & Schuster
Books for Young Readers

1230 Avenue of the Americas
New York, New York 10020

Book design by Heather Wood
The text for this book is set in Plantin.
Printed in the United States of America

2   4   6   8   10   9   7   5   3

Library of Congress Cataloging-in-Publication Data
Author talk : conversations with Judy Blume [et al.] / compiled and edited by Leonard S. Marcus.
p.   cm.
Summary: Presents interviews with fifteen well-known children's writers, including Judy Blume, Karen Cushman,
Russell Freedman, James Howe, Lois Lowry, Gary Paulsen, and Laurence Yep.
ISBN 0-689-81383-X
1. Children's literature, American—History and criticism—Theory, etc. Juvenile literature.
2. Authors, American—20th century Interviews Juvenile literature.
3. American literature—20th century—History and criticism Theory, etc. Juvenile literature.
4. Children's literature—Authorship Juvenile literature.
[1. Authors, American.   2. Authorship.]
I. Marcus, Leonard S., 1950-   . II. Blume, Judy.
PS490.A97 2000   810.9'9282--dc21   99-39777   CIP

Contents

Acknowledgments

I wish to thank the authors interviewed in this collection for their cooperation, interest, and patience, and for the many kindnesses they showed me as we worked together. In addition to the individuals and institutions named in the photo credits, I also wish to thank the following people for their help in verifying facts and securing illustrations and related material: Melanie Chang, Jennifer Flannery, Abby Williams Gese, Judith Haut, Kim Kahlhamer, Margaret Kimmel, Elizabeth Mahoney, Marilyn E. Marlow, John E. Peters, Andrew Pomes, Joanne Ryder, and Jonathan Ward. Finally, I express my appreciation to my editor David Gale, and to the staff of Simon & Schuster Books for Young Readers for their solid professionalism and unwavering good cheer, and to Andrea Davis Pinkney and Michele Coppola for their invaluable help and encouragement during the early stages of the making of this book.

Introduction

Fifteen authors are about to talk.

Some of these writers already may be among your favorite authors. Others may be new to you. But they all have remarkable stories to tell in the pages that follow—about their childhoods, and about people and places that have been important to them. They will talk about how they became writers, and about what it is like to be a writer.

If you were to gather together copies of every one of these authors' books, you would have quite a large and varied library. Within your library would be novels—some funny and some serious, and many that blend humor and seriousness in unexpected ways. There would also be poetry in your library, as well as short stories, picture books, plays, biographies, histories, memoirs, volumes of scientific fact, science fiction, and more. As you read the fifteen interviews in this book, you will discover that authors are every bit as different from each other as are the books they write.

Yet all fifteen writers also share important things in common. All have strong, clear memories of growing up. All can remember a time when they were not yet writers. All love their work. And all feel they are still learning about their craft.

An interview is a special kind of conversation. One person talks in response to another person's questions. Crafting an interview is something like painting a portrait in words: The interviewer tries to bring out "the essence" of his subject—to zero in on the telling details that make that person different from everyone else. To have a good interview, two things must happen: The subject must be willing to talk, and the interviewer must be ready to listen. By listening well, the interviewer will know when to ask the next question, and what to ask. If the conversation takes a surprising turn, the interviewer must be ready to follow.

I tape-recorded each of the interviews in this book, sometimes in person and sometimes by telephone. I then listened to the tapes over and over again before deciding which bits of conversation to keep, and which were not needed for these portraits. I next gave each author the chance to revise his or her answers, to choose their words with the utmost care, just as if they were writing—and rewriting—a manuscript.

Following each interview is a "Reader" or selected list of the author's work. I have indicated the publisher and year of publication of the first clothbound edition of a book followed (when applicable) by the publisher and year of the first paperback edition.

There are many ways to use and enjoy this book. If you are thinking about becoming a writer, you may find the advice or inspiration in these pages to get started. If you are curious about the life of a favorite author, you may find answers to some of your questions. If you do not have a favorite author, you may be about to discover one. Conversations like these can also add to the enjoyment of reading by reminding us, as Lee Bennett Hopkins has said, that "books are by people." Even the greatest classics are the work of men and women who once were young people.

Fifteen authors are about to talk.

Let's listen together.

Leonard S. Marcus

JUDY BLUME

(BORN FEBRUARY 12, 1938, ELIZABETH, NEW JERSEY)

Fans of Judy Blume tend to think of her not just as a favorite author but as a friend. The first fan letter Blume ever received, in 1971, came from a thirteen year old who wrote that in *Are You There God? It's Me, Margaret.* (1970) she had at last found a heroine she could identify with. Since then, a great many other readers have told the author of their surprise—and gratitude—at Blume's remarkable gift for knowing exactly what it is like to be them.

Blume is one of those rare writers who dared to write about things that had never been written about before. Her honest treatment of young peoples' feelings about sex broke the ice on a subject that had been largely ignored in earlier fiction for teens and preteens. Some adults were made so uncomfortable by this aspect of her writing that attempts were made to ban Blume's books at various schools and libraries. In response to the controversy, Blume became a strong advocate both for freedom of expression and for responsible sex education.

But Blume, who has two grown children and is now also a grandmother, never set out to become a "controversial" author. "I [have simply written]," she says, "the kinds of books that I wanted to read when I was young, books about real life and real feelings."

What kind of child were you?

Are You There, God? It's Me, Margaret. (1970)

Judy, at age 9

Up until I was about nine, I was shy and quiet like Sally in *Starring Sally J. Freedman as Herself* (1977). After that, I was more like Margaret in *Are You There God? It's Me, Margaret.* I always had an active fantasy life, fueled by movies. Following World War II, I fantasized about being a hero myself—a member of the Underground, fighting Hitler. Our family was Jewish, and I remember once being taken to the Bronx to meet a long-lost cousin who had survived the Holocaust by "living in a hole," as I was told. I began to wonder about this. *How could he have lived in a hole? What kind of hole was it? How did he eat and sleep and go to the bathroom in a hole? Was there a series of holes in which people lived? "My hole is next to your hole. We're neighbors...."* It was one of those things that a young child couldn't possibly understand, even though I knew it was all very serious and grim and had to do with being a Jew.

Did you have brothers or sisters?

I had one brother, David, who was four years older. David wasn't a parent pleaser, so that role fell to me.

We grew up in Elizabeth, New Jersey, where my father was a dentist. But when I was in the third grade, David became ill, and so my mother, my grandmother, and I went with David to stay in Miami Beach, where his doctors thought the climate would help him get better. We lived there for two school years, with my father visiting when he could. During those two years, I missed my father terribly and felt responsible for his well-being. Two of his older brothers had died at forty-two. The year that he turned forty-two was also the first year we were separated from him. I made numerous secret bargains with God, hoping to keep my father safe and healthy.

*It seems you had a very personal relationship with God,
even in your "Sally J. Freedman" days.*

I did. And by the time of my "Margaret" years, God and I were tight!

Did you enjoy school?

I always loved school.

Did you like to read?

My mother was a big reader, my father collected books, and so we had lots of books at home. I loved reading, too. As a preschooler, I discovered *Madeline* at the library. I loved it so much, I didn't want to part with it. In fact, because I thought I had the only copy in the world, I hid the book in my kitchen toy drawer so that my mother wouldn't be able to return it to the library. I knew it was wrong, but I couldn't give it up.

Later, I read Nancy Drew and the Oz books. But the first books that really spoke to me were the Betsy-Tacy books by Maud Hart Lovelace, which my mother bought for me. I loved the characters. They were alive for me. Betsy's family life seemed so wonderful, with their lively Sunday suppers and huge family gatherings.

Did you enjoy writing?

Yes. My classmates groaned when we got writing assignments, but I actually liked doing them. But in sixth grade, when we had to present book reports in front of the class, I didn't want to *report* on the books I was reading, so I made up books for my reports, coming up with a title, an author, a theme, and the major characters. I even made up an entire series of books about a horse named Dobbin, though I never actually read "horse" novels. I got a better grade on my invented book reports than when I'd actually read the book, but I remember having sweaty palms.

How did you imagine your future?

My father had led me to believe I could do anything I wanted. Early on, I pictured myself as having a life of adventure. My father's dreams for me were a lot like my own. He saw me on the stage and would have taken me to the best acting teachers. But by the time I was fourteen, I was identifying more with the reality that I would probably become a mother and wife, and maybe president of the PTA. This was the fifties, after all.

Tell me more about your "Margaret" personality change.

Following my two years in Miami Beach I had somehow become outgoing, interested (on the surface, anyway) in popularity and boys. By twelve I was reading the books I found on my parents' bookshelves—fiction by Saul Bellow, J. D. Salinger, and others. I had looked up sexuality in the *World Book Encyclopedia* a few years earlier and found only information about reproduction in plants. My answers to questions about sexuality, which my friends and I were desperate to have information about, came from fiction.

Did you, like Margaret, become curious about different religions?
Did you ever sneak into a confessional?

Oh, no!—though I *was* very curious about confession, which my Catholic friends would talk about. I wondered what went on in there. Years later, when I was seventeen, my brother married a Southern Baptist, and when they had children I wondered what it would be like for them not to grow up, as we had, with one religious tradition at home.

When did you decide to become a writer?

You don't write because you want to: You write because you have to.

I never decided. I was in my twenties and married with two kids when I received a brochure in the mail advertising a children's book-writing class at NYU, the college I had attended. I was already trying to do picture books, so I considered the brochure an omen. I signed up for that class and took a bus from New Jersey into the city one evening a week. The teacher was supportive and encouraging, and the next semester I took the course again. When I published two stories in little magazines, for twenty dollars each, I was thrilled. So was my teacher. Then I read an article about a new publisher called Bradbury Press that was interested in realistic fiction "for the eight-to-twelve set." So I sent them *Iggie's House* (1970), which I had written while taking the course. Dick Jackson, one of Bradbury's two editors, called, inviting me to come talk about the manuscript. During that meeting I learned that Bradbury wouldn't publish it as it was but was interested if I could rewrite it. We discussed the revisions—and I was so fired up, I went home and rewrote the whole book. Once I met Dick Jackson, everything fell into place. It was like "Sleeping Beauty": I had awakened, and from that time on, I wrote a book or more a year.

I think now of my first two books, *Iggie's House* and *The One in the Middle Is the Green Kangaroo* (1969), as exercises. When it came to writing my third book, *Are You There God? It's Me, Margaret.*, I thought to myself, *Okay. Now I know how to do it. This time I'm going to let go and write from deep inside what I know to be true about being eleven and twelve.*

> *Over the years I've learned to worry less that the words and ideas won't come. I trust that they will.*

What is a typical workday like for you?

When I'm working on a book, I eat my breakfast, get dressed, and go to work, pretending that I'm leaving the house and going to an office. I work until lunchtime. I force myself to sit at my desk. I might doodle a lot while I'm writing a first draft. Doodling is very important to me. I'll write down a word and decorate it. By the time I get to the end of a first draft, I have a good sense of the characters. During the next two rewrites I work longer hours and with more enthusiasm. By the third draft I'm so into the characters, I have to be dragged away from my desk.

How do you go about writing a book?

I start by filling a notebook with notes on characters—anything and everything that may never go into the book. This becomes my security blanket. Over the years I've learned to worry less that the words and ideas won't come. I trust that they will.

The more I write, the better I get to know my characters. I don't send a book to my editor until it's been through three go-rounds. Then, after talking with my editor, there is often another major revision, and then a polish.

Do you know from the start how a book will end?

I know the beginning—about the day when something different happens—and generally where the story's going. But how it will get there is what I worry about every time I begin a new book. I ask myself, *How am I going to fill up two hundred or three hundred pages!* But if I think of it as a whole book too soon, I'm going to scare myself. So I try to focus on one scene at a time. It may be just a page, it may be five or ten pages.

How do you know when it's time to send a manuscript to an editor?

I get to the point where I feel I can't do anything more without ruining it. That's when I finally show it to my editor, who can look at it freshly and help me make it better by asking the right questions.

Do you sometimes put stories about your own children in your books?

No. I've always felt that their lives were their own, so I have never really written about them, though the idea for *Blubber* (1974) grew out of an incident in my daughter's classroom. I feel the same way about my readers. When kids have asked me to write about something that happened to them, I've responded by suggesting that maybe they would grow up to write that book themselves, because it's their story to tell. I made one exception. I received a letter once from a twelve-year-old girl who was intellectually gifted and who said that she would give anything just to be a normal girl with friends. *Here's to You, Rachel Robinson* (1993) grew out of my interest in that girl.

A manuscript page from *Here's to You, Rachel Robinson* marked with the author's notations

What do you tell young people who want to write?

Don't let anybody discourage you. Lots of people tried to discourage me. And remember that you don't write because you want to: You write because you have to. You write from deep inside. And please don't be overly anxious to get published. It takes a lot of practice writing to become professional. We all have to pay our dues.

What is the best thing about being a writer?

One of the best things is that I get to play pretend all the time. And I like it when my characters surprise me. I'll say to my husband, George, "You won't believe what Rachel Robinson did today!" We talk about my characters at home as if they're real—because to me they are. But the very best thing about being a writer is hearing from so many people who say they feel connected to me through my characters.

A JUDY BLUME Reader
— — — — — — — — — — — — —

Are You There God? It's Me, Margaret. (Bradbury, 1970; Dell, 1972)

Blubber (Bradbury, 1974; Dell, 1976)

Deenie (Bradbury, 1973; Dell, 1974)

Forever . . . (Bradbury, 1975; Pocket, 1976)

Here's to You, Rachel Robinson (Orchard, 1993; Dell, 1994)

It's Not the End of the World (Bradbury, 1972; Dell, 1982)

Starring Sally J. Freedman as Herself (Bradbury, 1977; Dell, 1978)

Tales of a Fourth Grade Nothing, illustrated by Roy Doty (Dutton, 1972; Dell, 1976)

Then Again, Maybe I Won't (Bradbury, 1971; Dell, 1973)

Tiger Eyes (Bradbury, 1981; Dell, 1982)

*

BRUCE BROOKS

(BORN SEPTEMBER 23, 1950, WASHINGTON, D.C.)

Bruce Brooks feels "like a rookie," he says, every time he starts work on a new book. Writing for him is a kind of experiment. It is something like a sport: a chance to test—and stretch—his limits, sentence by sentence and word by word. He would rather have the self-doubt—and the edge—of a beginner, Brooks says, than write too easily, or know too definitely beforehand how a story will turn out.

Learning to start over was a big part of Brooks's childhood. Growing up in Washington, D.C., and in North Carolina, Brooks moved frequently after his parents divorced, when he was six. Transferring from school to school, he routinely found himself in the unenviable position of the "new kid" in class. He learned early on that his natural skill with words—whether expressed as a joke told to

schoolmates or a short story written for his own satisfaction—could be a lifesaver. He began to hone that skill as an athlete or musician might practice or train.

Brooks worked as a printer, reporter, and teacher before deciding to try his luck as a full-time writer. He was writing fiction at the time, but not for young readers. Then, an editor of adult fiction, to whom he had submitted his first novel, showed the manuscript to an editor in her company's children's book department. The children's book editor offered to publish the book, and Brooks accepted the offer. At first he was unsure whether he had made the right decision, but when children, teachers, and librarians embraced *The Moves Make the Man* (1984), Brooks knew he had found his audience.

What kind of child were you?

I was an only child, which meant that when I was alone I was really alone, and I was alone a lot. My parents were divorced when I was nearly seven. My mother, who was an alcoholic and a drug addict, and who suffered a series of nervous breakdowns, was often hospitalized. My stepfather was often at work or just not at home. I was often on my own after school and on into the evening. Often during those times I would wander around the cities I lived in, exploring.

My stepfather kept changing jobs, and as a result of this we moved so often that between second and eighth grades I never went to the same school for an entire year. All this change made me into a kind of jokester and a show-off. I needed to be noticed. And it made me very observant. I became a real spy and a quick study: On starting at a new school I could figure out right away who I wanted to make friends with, which kids I wanted to avoid. I noticed everything about everybody: when somebody got new sneakers or when somebody was sobbing quietly to herself. And I learned that you live the life you're given, and so I adjusted to whatever was going on around me.

Third-grade class photo

Did you enjoy reading?

I was very interested in comic books. Then, in fifth grade, a new teacher, in yet another new school, read to our class from books that weren't part of our schoolwork. The first was one of Beverly Cleary's novels about Beezus and Ramona. That was the first time I realized that school could be fun, and that books could be fun. That experience led me to read more on my own. In sixth grade, I read all the James Bond novels. In eighth grade, I read Charles Dickens's *Great Expectations*.

Did you like to write?

Very much. I started by trying to write comic books, but my drawing skills didn't keep pace with my writing and so after a while writing came to mean more to me. The word balloons took up more and more of the space. Eventually, I just drew tiny heads in the corner of each frame speaking my long sentences.

> *I would go over a passage again and again, trying to figure out why it moved me or made me laugh.*

At the same time, I realized that my stories weren't as good as the ones we were reading in school. So, much like the kids who were athletes or musicians, I practiced: I would pick a passage of description or dialogue from a book that interested me and go over it again and again, trying to figure out why it moved me or made me laugh. I did this for years. From the fifth grade on, I knew I eventually wanted to write novels.

Did any teacher, or other grown-up, praise your writing?

No, never. In 1957, when I was in second grade, the Soviet Union launched the first space satellite ever, *Sputnik I*, and Americans became terrified that our nation had fallen behind in math and science. As a result, schoolteachers encouraged kids to be math and science geniuses, not word geniuses. Being a scientist didn't interest me.

Your novel Midnight Hour Encores *(1986) is about a young musician. Did you enjoy music as a boy?*

I listened to music constantly, all kinds of music. During junior and senior high school, when I was living in Washington, D.C., which is a

Brooks, with his guitar, in his home office

largely African-American city, I got interested in black music, and went to black music stores and theaters that white people never went to. Dancing became very important to me then too.

Did you go in for sports?

I loved sports, but because we moved so much, I rarely got to play on a school team for a complete season. The other problem was that I was short for my age. But I was quick and a good passer. When I was living in Washington, D.C., an African-American friend who was six feet four used to go around with me to the playgrounds where black kids played serious basketball. I was accepted. We'd all kid around. And if I ever faked out one of the black players and sank a shot, they'd all laugh and say, "Oooh, white boy put the move on you!"

I loved sports in part because during a game, nothing else matters. Real time doesn't exist for the players. It doesn't matter that it is three o'clock; it only matters that three minutes remain in the game. I also liked the direct cause-and-effect of sports. If I faked a guy and hit a jump shot, well, that was something I had *done*. Outside of sports, I felt very much as though I couldn't make anything happen.

> *I always choose a project that I'm not sure I can pull off. I want to see if I can!*

Is that why you so often write about sports?

I don't know why. But as I began writing what became my first book, *The Moves Make the Man*, I found that I loved writing in Jerome's

anymore at all; she probably hadn't spoken in the room for a month. Instead, she
sank into the green chair and filled the room with the aroma of liquor that had
been metabolized.

Alice was appreciative of the fact that her mom never took a drink, even from her
nickel-plated hip-flask, in the room; she didn't wish to tell her mom she stank
almost as badly as the liquor would have, having taken the drink half an hour
before and given her body time to do whatever it did with alcohol on the cellular
level.

Her mother opened her purse and took out a magazine already rolled open to a
story. Glancing again at Alice, as if to make certain she wasn't sneaking a hot
dog on her watch, she crossed her legs and read her story. This is the way her
visits went, now; after half an hour of silent reading, she would put the magazine
back in her purse, stand up, walk over to plant a dry stinky kiss somewhere on
Alice's forehead, utter flatly the words "Try to eat something," then leave without
a backwards look.

Alice supposed her mom had reason to be angry. As she had put it shortly after
the girl announced her hunger strike and proved she was serious about it, "You
mean, essentially, you'd rather starve yourself to death than come into my home."

A manuscript page
from *Vanishing*

voice about basketball. That was the beginning. Later, writing about the imagined Little League game in *What Hearts* (1992) was a powerful experience for me. As the boy in that story rides in the car with his stepfather, he makes up an entire game, decides what happened in it, what didn't happen, and makes it all seem real. So that story isn't just about sports but is about the power of words, and of a child's imagination.

In the Wolfbay Wings hockey series, I set out to write twelve books—a "team" of books, as it were—each in a different teammate's voice. Those books aren't just about sports, either. The kids in those stories are building self-respect, which is basically what being a kid is all about. You're lucky if you're born with parents who encourage you to respect yourself, or if you stumble onto activities, like sports, in which you're given the chance to put yourself on the line.

Do you have a daily work routine?

I write twelve hours a day. I love to work—to figure things out. Until recently, I never had a special place to work. I wrote in hotel rooms, at this or that table, or on this or that couch. Now, however, I have a new desk and a new computer, and I expect that's where I will continue to write.

Do you revise your work much?

I think "revision" is badly named. The "re" prefix implies that you are going back over something you've already done. But you're not going back. You are going on with the writing process. It's all just part of getting it right. A friend of mine who played basketball once said that he envied me because he had just missed a foul shot that would have tied the score at the end of an important game. He said, "But you can write that foul shot until you make it." He was right. I write a first draft that I know is going to be partly good, partly bad. I may go over a manuscript three or four times before I'm satisfied.

What do you tell children who want to write?

To practice writing. To take your time and not expect to be able to write perfect stories. And to read analytically. Try, for instance, to write a paragraph describing a room that, without the use of a single negative adjective, makes the reader absolutely not want to go into that room. When you read a passage in a book that makes you feel sad or happy or scared, go back to it and ask yourself why.

What is the best thing about being a writer?

Writing books that at first seemed too hard to do. I always choose a project that I'm not sure I can pull off. I want to see if I can! I suppose it's like having to make that foul shot. It's a challenge, and I like the self-respect I gain from meeting a challenge well.

A BRUCE BROOKS Reader

Asylum for Nightface (Harper, 1996; Harper, 1999)

Boys Will Be (Holt, 1993; Hyperion, 1995)

Everywhere (Harper, 1990)

Making Sense: Animal Perception and Communication (Farrar, Straus & Giroux, 1993)

Midnight Hour Encores (Harper, 1986; Harper, 1988)

The Moves Make the Man (Harper, 1984; Harper, 1987)

Vanishing (Harper, 1999)

What Hearts (Harper, 1992; Harper, 1995)

The **Wolfbay Wings** series (Harper, 1997-1999)

KAREN CUSHMAN

(BORN OCTOBER 4, 1941, CHICAGO, ILLINOIS)

"Boring" was Karen Cushman's word, all through grade school, for history class. No wonder it was: Cushman's teachers treated the past as a long march of names and dates to be memorized and repeated back on tests. Years passed before she realized that history could also be the *story* of ordinary people's lives. Since making that discovery, history's stories have remained Karen Cushman's greatest passion as a reader and writer.

In college at Stanford, Cushman studied literature, classical languages, and archaeology. In the years after graduation, she worked in a variety of jobs, read widely, married, and moved from California to Oregon. Following the birth of her daughter, Cushman began reading children's books for the first time since she was a girl. Rediscovering the first books she had loved also stirred forgotten childhood longings to write. She began to have ideas for books, which she talked about until one day her husband finally dared her to write the book she had just described. Cushman accepted the challenge and spent the next three years researching and writing the story, in diary form, that became her triumphant first novel, *Catherine, Called Birdy* (1994).

What kind of girl were you?

Very bookish and imaginative and dreamy. I always had some fantasy going—a circus in the backyard, or a play in the garage, or a newspaper. After we moved from Chicago to southern California when I was ten, my mother and dad would say, "You always have your nose in a book. Go outside and play." So I would go outside—and be miserable until they let me back in so I could read some more.

Karen, at age 7, with her younger brother Duffy

How did you feel about moving?

I had mixed feelings. My parents tried to get me excited by saying that we could pick oranges all year round and go around barefoot. But I didn't want to leave behind my dog and my grandparents and my library.

Once you'd moved to California, what were some of the things you liked to do?

On hot summer days, my friends and I would sit on the curb waiting for women in high heels to pass by. We would watch as their heels sank into the melting asphalt.

Most of all, though, I liked to write. I wrote stories and plays. This must have started earlier because my parents had already given me a child's typewriter as a present when I was seven. I became known as the storyteller on our block. The neighborhood kids, all younger than me, would come to our house and lie on my bed, and

Karen, at age 12 (center, back), with Duffy (left) and neighbors

I became known as the storyteller on our block.

I would simply start, not knowing where my story would lead.

I was fifteen when the Elvis Presley craze began. I wrote an epic poem on the life of Elvis. I would also think up suggested plots for Elvis movies and send them in. I thought the movies being written for him were just terrible and that I could help. Of course I never heard back from him.

What did you like to read?

We didn't have a lot of books at home, but once I discovered the library, I was hooked. Sometimes I would start with the *A*s of a section and try to read my way through alphabetically. But then I'd get interested in another subject and switch to that section.

When did you decide to become a writer?

Not until much later. I didn't know any other kids who wrote, and certainly no adult who wrote for a living. I thought that when you grew up, you owned a gas station or got a job as a secretary.

Did you enjoy school?

No. I always did assigned reading the first week and then was bored all year. I hated history, which when I went to school was all about kings and things—memorizing names and dates. I was a grown-up when I discovered historical fiction. I became fascinated by that way of telling about history because it answered the question "What were they like?" It told what the people of another time wore, what they ate, where they went to the bathroom. Those were the kinds of things I really wanted to know!

How did you go about becoming a writer?

In college, I started out by majoring in English literature, then changed to classics—Greek and Latin. By then, I hadn't been doing any writing for a while. Sometime after college, the Middle Ages became a sort of hobby of mine. I would go to the Renaissance Fair, read books, and go to movies about the period. And when I somehow got the idea to write a story about a girl who was at odds with her culture, I thought, *How true that would have been in the Middle Ages, when girls wouldn't have had any power or value except economic value to their family.* I wrote my first book, *Catherine, Called Birdy*, as a series of relatively brief diary entries. I found writing in that structure much easier—and less intimidating—than writing a continuous narrative might have been.

> *You can't be a writer and a critic at the same time.*

Do you have a daily work routine?

I did at first. I would write every morning, take a break in the afternoon, then maybe write some more. As I have become more known, though, my schedule has become kind of crazy. I travel a lot, visiting schools and bookstores. I really enjoy those visits, but they make it harder for me to find the long, uninterrupted stretches of time that I need to travel back in time to write historical fiction.

Do you have a special place for writing?

I live in an old house and have an upstairs room with my desk and computer, lots of bookshelves, and windows overlooking a big tree in the backyard. I have all my girls on the walls: framed pictures of the covers of my books, and pictures of my daughter and her friends.

How do you go about writing a book?

I just keep writing. I tell myself, *It doesn't matter if it's awful: Get it*

Cushman's home office

all down on the page. Once I have my first draft, I go back to edit and revise.

What kind of research do you do?

By the time I wrote *Catherine*, I already knew a great deal about the Middle Ages, and when I wanted to learn more, I was able to find lots of books about everyday life during those times. I also read every historical novel for kids I could find; for instance, the beautiful novels about Roman Britain by Rosemary Sutcliff.

There weren't nearly as many books about the California gold rush, the period in which *The Ballad of Lucy Whipple* (1996) is set. In fact, the idea for *Lucy Whipple* came to me when I was browsing one day in the Oregon Historical Society's bookstore. I had picked up a book and read on the back cover that the gold rush was a "movement of men"—that ninety percent or more of the people who came to California to look for gold were men. Being a math wizard, I thought, *Okay, what about the other ten percent? What was it like for* them?

Do you know how a book will end right from the start?

I have a general idea. I'll write a paragraph-long summary before I start. But what actually happens between the first sentence and the last one often is a surprise.

Editorial comments on a manuscript page from *The Ballad of Lucy Whipple*

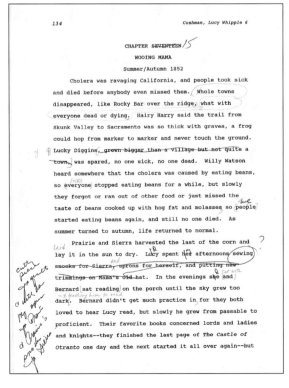

Is it hard to know when a book is done?

> After I've made my revisions and can't find anything else that needs changing, I send the manuscript to my editor. Inevitably, she finds lots more for me to do. Then the manuscript comes back to me. It may come back once—or three or four times. When neither of us can find anything more to revise, we call it finished. But a book is never really finished.

What do you tell young people who want to write?

> To read a lot and write a lot—that it's like exercising muscles. Also, to separate the writer from the critic. You can't be a writer and a critic at the same time. That is why I finish a draft before going back to edit. Otherwise, I might get too caught up in self-criticism, and never finish.

What is the best part about being a writer?

> I dedicated my first book, *Catherine, Called Birdy*, to my daughter and her five best friends. Watching them grow up together taught me a lot about girls—that girls can, for instance, be more independent-minded than I as a girl ever realized. They were an inspiration to me. As a writer, I in turn am glad to have the chance to inspire other girls.

A KAREN CUSHMAN Reader

The Ballad of Lucy Whipple

(Clarion, 1996; Harper, 1998)

Catherine, Called Birdy

(Clarion, 1994; Harper, 1995)

The Midwife's Apprentice

(Clarion, 1995; Harper, 1996)

RUSSELL FREEDMAN

(BORN OCTOBER 11, 1929, SAN FRANCISCO, CALIFORNIA)

What is a nonfiction writer? "A storyteller," Russell Freedman says, "who has taken an oath to tell the truth."

Growing up in San Francisco in a house full of books and lively conversation, Freedman always knew he would be *some* kind of writer. As a young person during the Great Depression, he saw first-hand the poverty and suffering of families less fortunate than his own. Years later, in his "photobiographies" *Franklin Delano Roosevelt* (1992) and *Eleanor Roosevelt* (1994), he recalled the era of his childhood as he chronicled the lives of two of that period's most compassionate leaders.

In his Newbery Medal-winning biography, *Lincoln* (1987), Freedman wrote about a hero whom he felt he had known almost personally since childhood. The author had been a somewhat mischievous schoolboy. A portrait of Lincoln hung in his principal's office. By the time he graduated, young Russell had spent many afternoons looking Abraham Lincoln in the eye.

After college and the army, Freedman took a job as a reporter and began to hone his writing skills in earnest. He published his first book, *Teenagers Who Made History* (1961), eight years later. Since then, he has written more than forty books, including natural science books as well as histories and biographies.

Freedman lives in New York, where the city's vibrant cultural life has proved an endless source of ideas. Museum exhibitions have inspired several of his books. When he began researching *Martha Graham* (1998), he was amazed to find that some of the original Graham dancers he hoped to meet were living in his own building! To interview them, Freedman recalls, ". . . all I had to do was take a short elevator ride and knock on their door."

What kind of boy were you?

I was a baseball fan. I loved books and history. And I always wanted to be a writer.

My father worked in the West Coast office of a major publishing company, Macmillan, and would invite the authors he met home for dinner. John Steinbeck; England's poet laureate, John Masefield; and Margaret Mitchell, the author of *Gone With the Wind*, all had dinner at our house. As a boy, I would sit at the table and watch and listen to those colorful, larger-than-life men and women. I wanted to be like them.

One writer who *never* came to dinner, though, was my favorite, a man named Howard Pease. Howard Pease wrote wonderful adventure stories about boys who ran away from home and sailed the world in the merchant marine. I read every book Howard Pease ever wrote. Then one day, when I was in the fifth grade, the most amazing thing happened. I heard that an author was coming to speak to our school,

> **The writer has to be able to feel the rhythm in the words.**

Russell (second row from the top, fifth from the left) in his fourth-grade class photo

and that that author was none other than Howard Pease! I was thunderstruck. I could hardly wait. Finally, the big day came. We went to the auditorium. Howard Pease spoke and autographed books. But the most amazing thing was that it turned out that he lived five blocks from me in San Francisco. I never got up the courage to knock on his door. But from that day onward, when I lay in bed at night listening to the foghorns by the Golden Gate Bridge, I would imagine that I *also* heard Howard Pease at his typewriter, just five blocks away, as he batted out his latest masterpiece.

How did you go about becoming a writer?

I entered contests as a kid. I wrote my own comic strip when I was in the fourth or fifth grade. I wrote short stories in high school. I won a prize in college, which was the first money I ever earned as a writer. My first job was as a reporter. The problem for me was finding out what kind of writer I could be. I had to learn that by trial and error.

Why do you find history so interesting?

History is the story of ourselves. It's the story of how we got to where we are today, and of the flesh-and-blood people who came before us and what they did—the people they loved, the wars they fought, the accidents they endured, the triumphs they enjoyed.

How do you choose the subjects of your biographies?

First of all, I choose a person I admire. I don't know if I would ever want to write about someone I didn't admire. Writing a biography takes a year of my life. It means in a sense that I live with that person for a year. I go to bed at night thinking about that person and I wake up in the morning thinking about him or her.

I also choose subjects whose lives have something to tell us about leading our own lives. I think of a biographical subject as a kind of teacher—for me and for my readers. A third consideration is that I don't like to get stuck in a rut. Crazy Horse, a mystic and a warrior, was an Oglala Sioux. Martha Graham, who invented an entirely new form of dance, spent her whole life living in Manhattan. No two people

> *The problem for me was finding out what kind of writer I could be. I had to learn that by trial and error.*

could be more different than Martha Graham and Crazy Horse. That was one of their appeals for me; another was that I admired them both.

Where do you get the photographs for your books?

To start with, I see photographs in other books about my subject. Then I begin my field research. I go to libraries and archives and search through boxes and boxes of pictures. For a book with fifty photographs, I might start by collecting three or four hundred.

Let's look at an old photograph from Children of the Wild West *(1983).* [See below.] *Why did you choose to include this one?*

It's a photograph, taken in the middle of the nineteenth century, of a pioneer school in Oregon. Oregon was a frontier community then, with widely scattered ranches and farms. The superintendent of schools for this particular rural district, Roy Andrews, would visit the schools on

From *Children of the Wild West*

horseback, taking along with him an old-fashioned box camera. He had one of the earliest cameras and must have been one of the first amateur documentary photographers of all time. He photographed the schools as he made his rounds.

I love this photograph because it shows so much about what a pioneer school and pioneer life were like. You can see the way girls dressed—in homemade hand-me-down "granny dresses." It's also interesting that their high-button shoes aren't very different from shoes that girls wear today, one hundred and fifty years later. This shows that fashions get recycled.

One of the girl's lunch boxes is an old tin that she probably got after her father used up the chewing tobacco that originally came in it. This illustrates the fact that everything had to be reused on the frontier. The other girl's lunch box is an old lard pail.

On the blackboard you can see the lesson plan. If anyone thinks that frontier schools were easygoing, just look at what they were studying. On Wednesday—history, arithmetic, geography, spelling. On Thursday—physiology, agriculture, grammar, reading. And these girls look to be in just the fifth or sixth grade.

But the best thing about the photo is that it's a timeless image. It's about two girls sharing a secret, in exactly the way that two girls would do so now, or would have done at any other time in the past.

> *It's impossible to write well about any subject without examining your own deepest feelings about it.*

Freedman at his desk in his New York City apartment

Do you have a daily work routine?

I write every morning. Because I'm lucky enough to work at home, I don't have to comb my hair before I go to work unless I feel like it.

People ask, "Do you write with a typewriter, or longhand, or with a computer?" You write with your mind. The rest doesn't matter. I happen to write my first draft longhand, with a pencil on a legal pad. I do this *because* it's slow: It gives me the time to think about what I'm doing. I type the next draft on an

A manuscript page from *Children of the Wild West*, with the author's revisions and a copy editor's marks

old-fashioned manual typewriter. It's an antique!—and I like the feel of it.

When you write, you want your work to have a certain rhythm. You want it to move, to carry the reader. You want the reader to feel swept along, as if on a kind of trip, from sentence to sentence. To do this, the writer has to be able to feel the rhythm in the words. It's when I retype a manuscript that I can tell how well it's moving and can spot passages where it gets bogged down. I type a manuscript at least four times.

How do you know when a book is done?

A book never really is finished. At some point you just have to say to yourself, I've done as well as I can do.

What do you like to do for fun?

Well, I love to write. When I'm working on a book, I write seven days a week. Of course, I also go to the movies and walk in the park and do other things. And when I finish a book I take a long vacation and often I'll take a trip to some exotic place. I've gone to a remote region of China to explore the foothills of the Himalayas, and to Australia to dive at the Great Barrier Reef. After one of these trips, I'm ready to dive into my next book.

What do you tell kids who want to write?

First, read what really interests you, no matter what it is, and when you come to a passage that affects you strongly, reread it and ask yourself why. And second, write every day. Keep a journal of your experiences. Test yourself on school assignments and letters to friends.

What is the best part about being a writer?

There are many best things. Being a nonfiction writer means that I can explore any subject that interests me. Being a writer means that I can explore myself: It's impossible to write well about any subject without examining your own deepest feelings about it. Also, writing, like carpentry, is a craft. It's very satisfying to make a beautiful object with your mind and hands. To write a good sentence that makes the reader see a picture vividly or feel an emotion strongly or dream a dream is a wonderful experience. To write a good book is a thrill.

A RUSSELL FREEDMAN Reader

Babe Didrikson Zaharias: The Making of a Champion (Clarion, 1999)

Buffalo Hunt (Holiday House, 1988; Holiday House, 1995)

Children of the Wild West (Clarion, 1983; Clarion, 1990)

Dinosaurs and Their Young, illustrated by Leslie Morrill (Holiday House, 1983)

Eleanor Roosevelt: A Life of Discovery (Clarion, 1993; Clarion, 1997)

Franklin Delano Roosevelt (Clarion, 1990; Clarion, 1992)

Immigrant Kids (Dutton, 1980; Puffin, 1995)

An Indian Winter, illustrated by Karl Bodmer (Holiday House, 1992; Holiday House, 1995)

Kids at Work: Lewis Hine and the Crusade Against Child Labor

(Clarion, 1994; Clarion, 1998)

Lincoln: A Photobiography (Clarion, 1987; Clarion, 1989)

Martha Graham: A Dancer's Life (Clarion, 1998)

*

LEE BENNETT HOPKINS

(BORN APRIL 13, 1938, SCRANTON, PENNSYLVANIA)

If a fortune-teller had predicted that Lee Bennett Hopkins would grow up to become a poet, the wiry, streetwise boy Hopkins was at twelve would have roared with laughter. Books and learning meant little to him as a child. When Hopkins's father, a policeman, deserted the family, their life spiraled downward into a dizzying scramble to pay the rent and keep food on the table. There were many days when Hopkins simply had no time for school.

An eighth-grade teacher finally persuaded him to care about learning and about his own future. Years passed before he became a writer, but it was that teacher's surprising "gift of hope," Hopkins says, that gave him his true start.

Hopkins has described his childhood in two novels, *Mama* (1977) and *Mama and Her Boys* (1981), and in a book of verse, *Been to Yesterdays* (1995). He has written several other books of poetry. He has also edited anthologies made up primarily of poems by others. Putting together an anthology about American heroes (*Lives: Poems About Famous Americans*, 1999) or about baseball (*Extra Innings*, 1993) is harder than it looks. The anthologist's work is like that of solving a puzzle, in which each poem serves as a unique piece on its way to becoming part of something larger. Hopkins may read thousands of poems in search of the right ones for a book of just twenty or thirty!

"Writing," Hopkins says, "is my life, my love!" And he roars with laughter at the thought that it is.

What kind of child were you?

Lee, at age 14

Horrible! I grew up in the projects in Newark, New Jersey, in an absolutely crazy home. My father left when I was fourteen, and my mother, who was very poor, had continued bouts with alcoholism. I rarely remember seeing her sober. We had no rules at home, and from early on I hated anyplace where there *were* rules—school, for instance. I grew up fast and developed street smarts because you had to in the projects to survive.

My childhood may sound like a disaster, but it wasn't all bad. I didn't want for very much because whatever we wanted, our mother stole for us! I had the best clothes, the best food. It was her way of survival.

Did you have brothers or sisters?

I was the oldest of three children and I literally had to raise my brother and especially our little sister.

Was there anything about school that you enjoyed?

No, nothing. And I wasn't good at anything there, either. School for me was a total nightmare.

How about reading?

I never read.

The original book jacket for *Mama*

Did any grown-up become important to you?

Early on, my grandmother—my mother's mother—did. She bounced me on her knee and recited nursery rhymes to me. I spent several summers with her. She was the stability in my life. Later on, my eighth-grade teacher, Ethel Kite McLaughlin, helped me. She saved my life. Mrs. McLaughlin apparently saw some talent in me and got me interested in the theater. That was it! Because of her, I began to read plays. I began to borrow records of Broadway musicals from the library and would sing along with them. When Mrs. McLaughlin told me about a nearby theater, the Paper Mill Playhouse, in Millburn, New Jersey, I saved my money and went to see my first live performance. It was the musical *Kiss Me, Kate*. That thrilling experience showed me there was more to life than the projects. From that day on I wanted to be a teacher like Mrs. McLaughlin. I felt that if she could save me, I could save other children.

Did you also begin to read other kinds of books, besides plays?

The first novel I ever read was *Little Women*. When I got to the last page I turned back to the beginning and started reading it again. This went on for about a year. I thought, *This is the book for me*. This is the family I never had. I didn't become a big reader until college, though. I was actually pretty lazy and mainly read *MAD* magazine, detective magazines, and DC Comics.

When did you become interested in poetry?

Not until I began teaching, in Fair Lawn, New Jersey, in 1960. I taught sixth grade for three years and worked as a "resource teacher" with students from kindergarten through sixth grade for another three years. I absolutely loved teaching. On my very first day, I clutched my briefcase so hard on my way to school that I cut my hand. That's how excited I was about teaching.

When did you begin writing and editing poetry books for children?

> *I wanted to be a teacher like Mrs. McLaughlin. I felt that if she could save me, I could save other children.*

That came about in the late 1960s. I first wrote articles for other teachers. I had left New Jersey by then and was working with African-American students in Harlem. They were a lot like me as a child. I wanted them to know the poetry of the great African-American poet Langston Hughes, and when I told the editor at a publishing house that there was no good book of Hughes's poetry for young readers, she asked me to edit one myself. *Don't You Turn Back: Poems by Langston Hughes*—the first book I edited—was published in 1969. A year later I accepted a job with Scholastic Inc., publishers of many good books for children and teachers. I was with Scholastic for seven and a half years. Since then I've been a full-time writer.

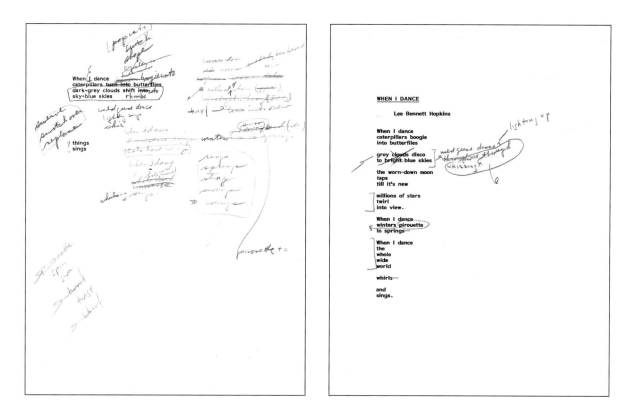

"When I Dance": from idea to the finished poem that appears in the book *Song and Dance*

What is a typical workday like for you?

I don't have a routine. I write whenever I feel like it. It's back to child-hood: no rules! Even so, I'm very disciplined. I'm always working on several books at a time. I always have a lot of projects going. I can write anywhere, but I work best at my home overlooking the Hudson River, where it's very quiet and I have my library and study. From my desk I can look directly out at the river. It's just gorgeous, ever-changing—and peaceful.

How do you write a poem? How do you get started?

A poem usually starts with an image, something I've seen on a walk—a nest of young pigeons, for instance. When I first moved out of the city I knew nothing about nature. I thought all birds were pigeons. I saw a blue jay one day and I thought it must be a blue pigeon. I thought, *I didn't know they came in colors!*

> **WHEN I DANCE**
>
> When I dance
> caterpillars boogie
> into butterflies
>
>   wild geese disco
>   lighting up
>   skies
>
> the worn-down moon
> taps
> till it's new
>
>   millions of stars
>   twirl
>   into view
>
> When I dance
> winters
> pirouette
> to springs—
>
>   When I dance
>   the
>   whole
>   wide
>   world
>
> whirls—
>
> and
> sings.
>   — *Lee Bennett Hopkins*

Do you revise much?

Sometimes a poem comes to me full-blown—right away. Other times, I work on one for months and months. Some poems remain unfinished for years.

What do you do when you get stuck and don't know what to write next?

I go to Saks Fifth Avenue, look at the price of Ultrasuede jackets, and tell myself, *You'd better get back to it, guy, or you're not going to be able to afford anything like that!* I'm a professional. If I hit a problem, I work it out because I know I've got to.

How do you know when a book is done?

There just comes a time when I know I've done the best I can do, and then I let it go.

What do you tell girls and boys who want to write?

I thought all birds were pigeons. I saw a blue jay and I thought, I didn't know they came in colors!

I get letters from students who say they want to be poets. That's so exciting, I can't stand it. I tell them to read, that they're not going to become writers if they're not readers. I encourage them to read the best poets—John Ciardi, David McCord, Myra Cohn Livingston, Valerie Worth, Lilian Moore, and others. One reason poems are good to read is that they are often quite short. And it's wonderful to realize that more can sometimes be said and felt in eight or ten lines of a poem than can be said and felt in an entire novel.

What else do children ask you?

One child asked if I have a poetic license on my car! Isn't that wonderful? Since *Been to Yesterdays*, which is a book of poems about my own growing up, was published, children ask me all sorts of personal questions. Did my mother drink? Did my father beat me? He didn't, in fact. How did I survive? Many children today lead horrendous lives. They are looking for the courage and strength to go on. I tell them that I hated school but that one teacher helped me and that if it wasn't for my education, I don't know what would have happened to me.

What is the best thing about being a writer?

To have written! Today I almost had tears in my eyes. I was walking down the street in Greenwich Village, and there was a little girl coming out of school with her mother, carrying a copy of *Amelia Bedelia*. I knew and loved the author, Peggy Parish, and as I looked at that girl holding a book that was originally published in 1963, I thought, *It's amazing. Books really do go on forever and ever!*

A LEE BENNETT HOPKINS Reader

Been to Yesterdays: Poems of a Life, illustrated by Charlene Rendeiro

(Boyds Mills, 1995; Boyds Mills, 1999)

Don't You Turn Back: Poems by Langston Hughes (editor),

illustrated by Ann Grifalconi (Knopf, 1969)

Extra Innings: Baseball Poems (editor),

illustrated by Scott Medlock (Harcourt Brace, 1993)

Hand in Hand: An American History Through Poetry (editor),

illustrated by Peter Fiore (Simon & Schuster, 1994)

Lives: Poems About Famous Americans (editor),

illustrated by Leslie Staub (HarperCollins, 1999)

Mama, illustrated by Stephen Marchesi (Knopf, 1977; Boyds Mills, 2000)

Mama and Her Boys, illustrated by Stephen Marchesi (Harper, 1981; Boyds Mills, 2000)

Pauses: Autobiographical Reflections of 101 Creators of Children's Books

(Harper, 1995)

Rainbows Are Made: Poems by Carl Sandburg (editor),

illustrated by Fritz Eichenberg (Harcourt Brace, 1982; Harcourt Brace, 1984)

Song and Dance, illustrated by Cheryl Munro Taylor (Simon & Schuster, 1997)

✳

JAMES HOWE

(BORN AUGUST 2, 1946, ONEIDA, NEW YORK)

James Howe had the kind of parents who do their best to encourage their children's creativity. When young James constructed an elaborate building-block city across the expanse of the Howe family's living room floor, their comment was, "Isn't that wonderful!"—not, "Clean up that mess!" They laughed at his jokes, typed the stories he dictated when he was still too young to write them down, and did not say "no" when, as a college-bound teenager, Howe spoke of his determination to become an actor. They simply urged him to prepare for a teaching career, too, should stardom never come his way.

The actor's life did prove too hard for him. Several years and career changes after graduating from college, Howe and his wife, Deborah, began writing, just for fun at first, the story that became *Bunnicula: A Rabbit-Tale of Mystery* (1979). It was their first children's book and first collaboration as writers. Sadly, Deborah Howe became ill and died before *Bunnicula* was published.

It was difficult at first, but Howe continued to write for children on his own. One reason that he still enjoys doing so is that writing his dialogue-filled books is in some ways not very different from acting. Howe often talks to himself as he works. If he reaches a particularly tough spot in a story, he may even get up from his desk, pace the room, and act out the scene that is giving him trouble. Taking all the parts— dog, cat, rabbit, human, or whatever—Howe *becomes* his characters, and he does not stop talking until he knows what they have to say.

Third-grade school photo

What kind of child were you?

I was silly and I was serious. I was like two pieces of a puzzle that didn't quite fit together. I loved joking and wordplay and just playing. But I was also very sensitive to the world around me. I paid attention. I could be shy in groups or with new people, but I also loved getting up onstage and acting. I loved to perform.

My book *Pinky and Rex and the School Play* (1998) is largely based on an experience I had in the fourth grade. Our class was putting on a play set in the jungle. I had my heart set on playing the lead but was instead cast as a monkey. I felt doubly humiliated because, although I was supposed to be a monkey, I ended up having to wear my leftover Halloween costume—a gray cat suit! I had my moment in the sun, however, when at one point during the performance the other kids all simply forgot to stand up in unison on cue. I saw this happening and thought, *Hey, I'm a monkey. I can go anywhere and do anything I want!* So I started bounding across the stage and whispering into everyone's ear, "Stand up! Stand up! Stand up!" Everyone stood up, and the audience applauded!

Did you have brothers or sisters?

I was the youngest of four brothers—the next youngest was eight years older than me. That is probably one of the reasons why I loved *Charlotte's Web*, which my parents gave me when I was in first grade. Like Wilbur the pig, I was the runt of the litter. I think I identified with his need to survive as the little one in a big world, and to find his own way. I loved the book so much that I immediately brought it in to school for my teacher—whose name just happened to be Miss Wilbur!—to read to our class. Fortunately, she had a great sense of humor.

> **What fascinated me most about [Charlotte's Web] was that the animals had their own world.**

I became drawn to humor in part as a way of impressing my older brothers. I borrowed joke books from the library and would come to the dinner table armed and ready. At dinner, my brothers and my father, who was a minister and a wonderful preacher, would talk and talk and talk. Hardly a sentence went by without someone picking up on a word and taking it in some other direction. My mother wasn't good at wordplay but was a very appreciative audience. She'd laugh so hard, she'd sometimes have to run out of the room, clutching her sides because they were aching so much.

Did you enjoy school?

I loved school and was an excellent student, especially in English. I won every spelling bee until the seventh grade. I was good at math but had to work hard at it. But I was no good at gym or science. Looking back, the teachers I liked best were the ones who asked the most of me. By having high expectations of me, they helped me see myself as someone who was smart and capable of working harder and accomplishing more than I thought I could.

What books besides Charlotte's Web *did you like to read?*

I was a very slow reader and at first read mostly comic books, *MAD* magazine, and comic strips, of which *Peanuts* was my favorite. Then, in sixth grade, I discovered adult literature and became an avid reader, though still a slow one.

Were you interested in writing?

I was always writing stories and poems. In the fifth grade I wrote a play that I put on with my friends. It was called *Dagwood's Awful Day* and was based on the *Blondie* comic strip. I directed it, played the starring role, and sold lemonade during intermission.

Did you always want to become a writer?

Growing up in upstate New York, I got to ride horses. When I was very young, I wanted to be a jockey. But, as my mother pointed out, with all the six footers in our family, I was likely to be too tall for that. She was right; I grew up to be six feet two.

At ten, I decided to become an actor. I was very serious about it. My childhood hero was the great English actor Laurence Olivier! I was probably the only ten-year-old boy around who enjoyed shutting himself up in his bedroom to listen over and over to recordings of Olivier performing *Hamlet* and *Richard III*. I took a book on acting out of the public library so many times in two years that when I moved at the age of twelve, the librarian gave it to me! I still have it.

That goal—of becoming an actor—carried me through college, where I majored in theater. My parents were encouraging, always taking me to plays—and then backstage to get the actors' autographs. But they also wanted me to prepare for more practical work, like teaching.

Did you act professionally?

Not for very long. I acted in some off-off-Broadway and summer stock productions, appeared in several commercials, modeled for magazine ads, and was an extra in a handful of movies. I didn't make much of a living at it. In time, I became more interested in directing and pursued that, but it was still a struggle to make money.

When did you become a writer?

In my late twenties. My late wife, Debbie, and I wrote our first children's

Bunnicula costume

book, *Bunnicula*, almost by chance. Debbie and I enjoyed watching late-night vampire movies on TV and would laugh at how ridiculous those horror movies often really were. That somehow prompted me to think up the silliest kind of vampire I could possibly imagine—and that is when "Count Bunnicula," a fluffy little bunny with fangs, first occurred to me. But I had no thought then of writing a book. Two years later, Debbie happened to mention Count Bunnicula one day to her mother, who—instead of suggesting I see a psychiatrist!—said, "That sounds like a wonderful character for a children's book." That night after dinner Debbie and I sat down at the kitchen table with a writing pad and started brainstorming the characters and story ideas. We were just having fun with it at first, but eventually I showed the manuscript to some publishers, one of whom liked it and offered to publish it. Writing *Bunnicula* brought me back to *Charlotte's Web*. As a child, what most fascinated me about E. B. White's book was the idea that the animals could have their own world and communicate with each other. The animals in *Bunnicula* also have that secret kind of other life when the humans leave the room.

Do you have a daily work routine?

I vary what I do. I work better in the afternoon and evening than I do in the morning. I aim for four hours of solid writing in a day. If I can do more than that—all the better! Usually, I write at home, where it is quiet. But sometimes I want to be among people while I'm working and so I will go into Manhattan and write in a coffee shop or museum or library.

Howe, in his home office

How do you go about writing a book?

I start with an idea I've jotted down in a notebook. I have file folders full of ideas. If the idea catches fire, I'll develop it by writing in longhand whatever occurs to me—just letting my mind float. I ask myself lots of "what if?" questions: *What if the rabbit attacks vegetables instead of people? What if the girl is painfully shy? What if she's shy because she's afraid of something? What might she be afraid of?* At a certain point I know I've done enough of what I call "prewriting" and realize it's time to start writing the story. That is always the hardest time for me. By then, I may know the story I want to tell but not *how* I want to tell it. In some ways it's like putting on a play. In the theater, you have to think carefully about what you want the audience to see first, when the curtain goes up. That first impression matters. Similarly, when I'm writing I have to decide at precisely what moment the story should begin and what image and mood I'm creating for the reader with those first words. Final impressions are also important. I usually know how my story will end early on in the writing. Getting there is the hard part!

> *Writing is like digging in the sand for buried treasure:*
> *You have to be willing to do a lot of digging.*

Do you revise your work much?

I love to revise. I guess it's the theater director in me: I enjoy taking something that exists in raw form and seeing how I can shape it.

James and Deborah Howe's first notes for *Bunnicula*

What do you tell children who want to write?

To read and write. As a child I learned how to build humor by reading *Peanuts.* Also, be patient with yourself and don't expect everything you write to be wonderful. Writing is like digging in the sand for buried treasure: You have to be willing to do a lot of digging. Most of what you unearth won't glitter. But there are treasures to be found in your imagination. Just keep digging, and they'll reveal themselves.

What do you like to do when you are not working?

I like to go to the theater and movies and concerts. I also like to read and to draw; to go biking and to bake anything with chocolate! And I enjoy spending time with my daughter.

What is the best part of being a writer?

Those moments when I write something really powerful—something that affects me strongly, makes me laugh or brings tears to my eyes or makes me see something differently than I've seen it before. And all because of what I've done with a few words. Words are so powerful. They're tools we use for digging and, at the same time, they're the treasure waiting to be found.

A JAMES HOWE Reader

Bunnicula: A Rabbit-Tale of Mystery (coauthored by Deborah Howe), illustrated by Alan Daniel (Atheneum, 1979; Avon, 1980)

The Hospital Book, illustrated with photographs by Mal Warshaw (Crown, 1981; Beech Tree, 1994)

Howliday Inn, illustrated by Lynn Munsinger (Atheneum, 1982; Avon, 1983)

Morgan's Zoo, illustrated by Leslie Morrill (Atheneum, 1984; Avon, 1986)

A Night Without Stars (Atheneum, 1983; Avon, 1985)

Pinky and Rex, illustrated by Melissa Sweet (Atheneum, 1990; Avon, 1991)

The Watcher (Atheneum, 1997; Aladdin, 1999)

What Eric Knew (Atheneum, 1985; Avon, 1986)

✳

JOHANNA HURWITZ

(BORN OCTOBER 9, 1937, NEW YORK, NEW YORK)

The first time Johanna Hurwitz saw her name in print, it was not in the pages of a book or a magazine but on a bedspread. An aunt had embroidered JOHANNA across her young niece's tan bedcover in large, looping letters of bright red wool. Hurwitz recalls running her fingers over the bold, bright lines that formed her name. "There was something quite mysterious and exciting to see the word spelled out and to learn that a written word could represent a person. Me." The novels that Hurwitz grew up to write brim with many such surprising homegrown discoveries.

Hurwitz realized one of her childhood dreams—that of becoming a librarian—years before she realized the other, and became an author. When her first book, *Busybody Nora*, was published in 1976, she was still working as a school librarian. While "weeding" the library shelves one day of books too old and battered to keep, she came across a tattered copy of a novel by one of her own favorite childhood authors, Carolyn Haywood, creator of the Betsy and the Little Eddie series. By a delightful coincidence, Haywood's lifelong publisher, William Morrow and Company, was now also Hurwitz's. Valentine's Day was fast approaching, and this gave Hurwitz an idea. She knew that authors see their own books when they are brand-new—before anyone has had a chance to handle them. And she knew that in libraries the best-loved books are always those that receive the

most wear and tear. She wanted Carolyn Haywood to see how well-loved her stories still were by the children at her library. So Hurwitz wrapped the book in bright red holiday paper, enclosed a card, and dropped the parcel in the mail—a valentine surprise from one author to another.

What kind of child were you?

I was shy and very quiet at school. At home, though, where I was the oldest child, I was much more outgoing. I would, for instance, make up stories for my younger brother about his two favorite things: bananas and chocolate. I liked having the power to cast a spell over him.

Johanna, on her eleventh birthday

Did you enjoy reading?

I loved reading. My father once owned a secondhand book store in New York City. Years later Mother worked at the New York Public Library. Our small Bronx apartment was filled with books. *Anne of Green Gables*, *Heidi*, and *Stuart Little* were favorites, as were the Nancy Drew series and Lois Lenski's regional books, and, best of all, the Betsy-Tacy series. I reread Laura Ingalls Wilder's *The Long Winter* every summer. In the sweltering Bronx heat, that book about plunging temperatures was my interior air-conditioning.

> *I don't make a detailed outline because to get to the ending is part of the adventure for me.*

When I had to read out loud in school, however, I would become so nervous about possibly mispronouncing a big word that I often stumbled on the easy words that came before it. As a result, I was never in the top reading group.

Did you enjoy writing?

Oh, yes. Our local library had a reading club for fifth- and sixth-grade girls, for which I wrote stories that the librarian read out loud. She also copied my stories in her beautiful handwriting and pasted them into a scrapbook. That was lovely. More often, though, I was a closet writer. I didn't try out for my high school newspaper because I was afraid that the other kids wouldn't like my kind of writing.

One thing that I especially liked about the Betsy-Tacy books was that the author, Maud Hart Lovelace, had written about her own Minnesota childhood: She *was* Betsy. At first I thought this meant that I, too, should write stories set in Minnesota, even though I had never been there. Later, I found a better lesson in her example: I realized that when I grew up I could write about my life in New York City. Starting with my first book, *Busybody Nora*, that is what I did. *Once I Was a Plum Tree* (1980) is the most autobiographical of my books.

What was it like growing up in the Bronx during World War II?

Scary. Even though the fighting never came close to us, we didn't know for sure that it never would. I would lie in bed at night, hearing airplanes overhead, and wonder if the Bronx was about to be bombed. Now when I hear an airplane I sometimes think, *Isn't it nice to be able to hear that sound and not be frightened?* During the war, I had a little box in which I kept a small doll and a few other treasures. I kept my box ready to take with me if we ever had to leave our apartment in a hurry. I had another box with Band-Aids so that if an injured pilot happened to parachute down onto our block, I'd be able to bandage him up and rescue him.

When did you decide to become a writer?

I always wanted to write. My parents, however, told me that I would never earn a living that way, so I decided to become a librarian, too.

Was there one librarian you especially looked up to?

I met Frances Clarke Sayers, the head of children's services at the New York Public Library, when I was twelve. I had written her a letter asking what the advantages and disadvantages were of being a librarian. She wrote back inviting me to come for a visit. Mrs. Sayers was also a children's book author, so she was a wonderful role model for me.

How did you go about becoming a writer?

After working at the New York Public Library for several years, which was a great learning experience, I became the librarian at the Calhoun School, a private school in New York City. That's when I wrote my first book, *Busybody Nora*. I sent the manuscript to publishers for three years before William Morrow finally accepted it. There were four chapters originally, each of which was a short story that stood on its own. My editor asked me to write two more stories to complete the book. By the time *Busybody Nora* was published, I had written my second book, *Nora and Mrs. Mind-Your-Own-Business* (1977). Even so, I was still feeling a little unsure of myself. Then my editor said a very good thing to me: "You're one of us now." That's when I really knew that being a writer was not just a fantasy anymore.

What is a typical workday like for you?

> *I would make up stories for my younger brother. I liked having the power to cast a spell over him.*

I start my day by taking a walk. Walking clears my head, and I'll sometimes suddenly realize the solution to a problem in the book I'm writing. After my walk, I come home, have breakfast, and write until one. If the telephone rings, I jump up and answer it. It's sometimes nice to be distracted. After lunch, I'll do neighborhood errands and answer the mail.

When I'm working well, I become lost in thought—a wonderful feeling. Once, while writing on my laptop onboard a plane, I even forgot where I was. When the stewardess came by to offer me a beverage, I looked up and all I could think was, *What is this lady doing in my study?*

How do you go about writing a book?

When I start, I know the beginning and the ending but not what will happen along the way. I don't make a detailed outline because to get to the ending is part of the adventure for me. I don't want to feel that I'm simply following a map.

My characters sometimes surprise me. As I began writing *Much Ado About Aldo* (1978), for instance, I knew that Aldo was a boy who loved animals and that he would be upset about chameleons eating the crickets that his class was raising. But I didn't know he was going to be a vegetarian. It was as though Aldo said to me, "How can I be upset about crickets if I eat chicken for dinner?" Aldo told me.

What do you do when you get stuck and don't know what to write next?

When I was having trouble making progress with *Spring Break* (1997), I decided as a kind of experiment to start with the last chapter and write the book backward. To my delight, it worked. But I don't plan to write all my books backward.

Do you put stories from your children's lives into your books?

All the time. In *Superduper Teddy* (1980), the mother takes Teddy to a birthday party. Lots of kids are already there when they arrive, and when Teddy shyly pulls back from the door, the mother says, "Go on, Teddy. Those are all your friends in there." But it turns out that those *aren't* his friends: It's the wrong party. That happened to us when a doorman sent my son Ben and me to the wrong floor of an apartment house where more than one birthday party was in progress.

I've also gotten ideas from children on school visits. Once in Alaska a boy suddenly stuck his head through the opening in a chair. That set me to thinking, *What if he got stuck? What kind of a kid would do this sort of thing? What else might he do?* Before I knew it, I was writing *Class Clown* (1987).

Manuscript page from *A Llama in the Library*, with editor's queries on yellow flags

Do you revise much?

> All the time.

How do you know when a book is finished?

> I know when *I* think it's done. But that doesn't mean my editor will agree. If something is missing from the story, my editor will point it out by asking me a question.

What do you tell kids who want to write?

> To read and write: Keep a journal or diary or have pen pals. The more you write, the better you'll become. It's the same as with Olympic athletes. Not one of them decided to become an athlete just two weeks before the Games. They've worked for years, had failures, but stuck with it and believed in themselves.

What do you like to do when you are not working?

> Read. Visit secondhand bookstores, where you never know what books you'll find. Go to Mets games. Explore back roads with my husband

Hurwitz, at her summer home in Vermont

near our summer home in Vermont. Now that I'm a grandmother, I've taken up knitting again, which I last did when I was a kid. I'm amazed that I can take some wool, two little sticks, do something with them— and out comes a sweater.

What is the best thing about being a writer?

One of the best things is knowing that books take on a life of their own, that my stories can touch children I'll never meet in places where I'll never go. I also like writing fiction because it's a little bit like being God: Nothing happens in a story unless I want it to happen. That's why most of my books have happy endings: What's the use of having that power unless it's to make good things happen?

A JOHANNA HURWITZ Reader

The Adventures of Ali Baba Bernstein, illustrated by Gail Owens

(Morrow, 1985; Avon, 1995)

Anne Frank: Life in Hiding, illustrated by Vera Rosenberry

(Jewish Publication Society, 1988; Beech Tree, 1993)

Busybody Nora, illustrated by Susan Jeschke

(Morrow, 1976) / reillustrated by Lillian Hoban (Morrow, 1990; Puffin, 1991)

Class Clown, illustrated by Sheila Hamanaka (Morrow, 1987; Scholastic, 1995)

A Llama in the Library, illustrated by Mark Graham (Morrow, 1999)

Much Ado About Aldo, illustrated by John Wallner (Morrow, 1978; Puffin, 1989)

Nora and Mrs. Mind-Your-Own-Business, illustrated by Susan Jeschke

(Morrow, 1977; Dell, 1981) / reillustrated by Lillian Hoban (Morrow, 1991; Puffin, 1991)

Once I Was a Plum Tree, illustrated by Ingrid Fetz (Morrow, 1980; Beech Tree, 1992)

Spring Break, illustrated by Karen Dugan (Morrow, 1997; Beech Tree, 1999)

Superduper Teddy, illustrated by Susan Jeschke

(Morrow, 1980; Dell, 1982) / reillustrated by Lillian Hoban (Morrow, 1990; Puffin, 1991)

E. L. KONIGSBURG

(BORN FEBRUARY 10, 1930, NEW YORK, NEW YORK)

A good novel, E. L. Konigsburg once observed, is like a cone of fudge ripple ice cream. "You keep licking the vanilla, but every now and then you come to something darker and deeper and with a stronger flavor." The best stories, in other words, combine sheer enjoyment with food for thought.

Elaine Konigsburg was always a good reader. But as a child grow-

ing up during the Great Depression she did not imagine that she might one day write books of her own. The first member of her family ever to attend college, she worked her way through school while majoring in chemistry, a "practical" field in which she excelled and in which she knew she could eventually find a job.

Konigsburg graduated with honors, married a psychologist, and studied chemistry for two more years before taking a job teaching science at a private girls' school. She left teaching when the first of her three children was about to be born. In the years that followed she took art classes and then decided—keeping it a secret at first from all but her family—to try her hand at writing stories for children. Remarkably, she published her first two novels in the same year, 1967. One of those first two novels, *From the Mixed-Up Files of Mrs. Basil E. Frankweiler,* won the most prestigious literary prize given to an American children's book, the Newbery Medal. Still more remarkably, Konigsburg's other novel for 1967, *Jennifer, Hecate, Macbeth, William McKinley, and Me, Elizabeth,* won the second most important prize, a Newbery Honor. Konigsburg illustrated both novels herself. All in all, it was an amazing new beginning for one who had long imagined for herself a future filled not with words and pictures but equations, metric measures, and the odd laboratory explosion.

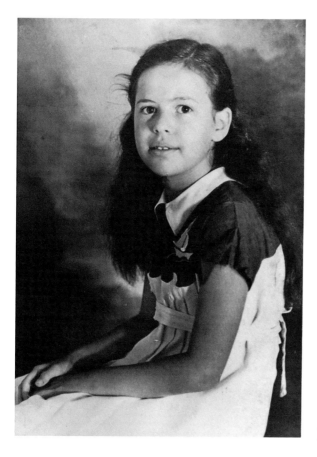

Elaine, at age 10

What kind of girl were you?
Serious. Timid. A good student—that was the way I could make my mark.

Did you have favorite subjects?
Anything that did not involve music or sports. I was hopeless at both. All through elementary school, our classes were divided into redbirds and bluebirds. The bluebirds were allowed to sing; the redbirds listened. I was a redbird. At Christmas redbirds were allowed to sing, but carols were all that was offered. Being Jewish, I did not think I should sing, but I wanted to, so I did. But when I came to the words "Jesus" or "Christ," I hummed. Fortunately, gym and music were never given letter grades. (How could anyone give a redbird a grade when she was never allowed to sing?) When I was in ninth grade, I had my first course in general science, and I developed a deep interest in that subject. I was in love with logic at the time.

What did you do for fun?

I liked to draw, and I loved going to the movies. My favorite movies were the ones starring Ginger Rogers and Fred Astaire, and historical epics like *Marie Antoinette*. Until I was ten, we lived over my father's store on the main street of town, and we played sidewalk games like Statue, May I?, and Hopscotch, and we could roller-skate when the stores were not busy. Indoors we played Pick-up Sticks, Chinese Checkers (I was good at it), Jacks (never got past twosies), and lots of cards.

Did you enjoy reading?

Oh, yes. My mother and father never cared what I read, but they did care *when* I read. I used to have what my family called "dishes diarrhea." Whenever there were dishes to be done, Elaine would have to go to the bathroom. The bathroom was the only room in the house with a lock on the door, and I used to go there to read. I read a lot of trash—*True Confessions* magazines and that sort—which I hid in the clothes hamper. I remember crying so hard as I read the final chapters of *Gone With the Wind* that I kept flushing the toilet so that my parents wouldn't hear me.

What was it like growing up during the Great Depression?

As a child, I never found any characters in books whose lives resembled those of my classmates, my family, and me.

The books I read as a child, such as *Mary Poppins* and *The Secret Garden*, were about people who had maids and spoke beautifully polished English. In contrast to this, in our Pennsylvania mill town, people during the Depression were hiring out as maids, and my father lost a business. Some of my school friends spoke with foreign accents because they had learned English from immigrant parents who spoke with foreign accents. As a child, I never found any characters in books whose lives resembled those of my classmates, my family, and me. Years later, this made me want to write for children about things as they are—about people and places that my own children would recognize as real.

How did you go about becoming a writer?

Aside from the fact that I have always been a reader—even as I majored in chemistry at Carnegie Mellon University—I have had only one formal writing course. As a freshman I was required to take a course in English composition that was designed to teach us to write about complicated processes in a simple, straightforward fashion. To this day, I cannot think of better training for a writer of children's books.

Are there some ways in which writing fiction is like being a scientist?

Both require discipline—and imagination. Einstein and Darwin could make their giant leaps because they asked the right questions. Giant leaps like theirs are made in the imagination.

Why did you not become a chemist, after all?

I was in graduate school at the University of Pittsburgh when my husband finished his doctorate and found a position in Jacksonville, Florida. I had completed my course work but not the research project for my graduate degree. I detested the lab work—washing all those beakers and three-neck, round-bottom handblown flasks with ground-glass, custom-fitted stoppers that cost a gazillion dollars each and that had a bad habit of blowing up on me. I hated the smells and having to weigh everything down to the thousandths of a gram—called "milligrams," if I recall. Besides, it's hard to measure what you spill, and I spilled a lot. In a lab you have not only to measure everything—time, temperature, color, amount—you have to keep track of it all in fractions. I left graduate school to move with my husband to Florida. There was not then—and there is not now—a place where a person can get a graduate degree in organic chemistry in Jacksonville, so I took a position teaching science at a private girls' school. I have never regretted my education in science, and I have never regretted leaving the lab.

> *Kids want to be like everyone else and they want to be different from everyone else.*

When did you write your first book?

When the third of my three children started kindergarten. We had moved from Jacksonville, Florida, to the suburbs of New York in the early 1960s, from the soft, gentle, mannerly suburbs of the South to the brisk, bustling suburbs of the Northeast, but the regional differences did not matter because there was much more that was alike in my children's lives than was different. I realized then that they were a genre: middle-class suburban. I wanted to see their lives documented in fiction because—strangely enough for a student of science to say—reading about it adds a measure of reality for me.

Why do you write so often for children of about the age of twelve?

Because it is at that age that the serious question of childhood is asking for an answer. Kids want acceptance from their peers, but in two different, opposing ways: They want to be like everyone else and they want to be different from everyone else. So the question is: How do you reconcile these opposing longings?

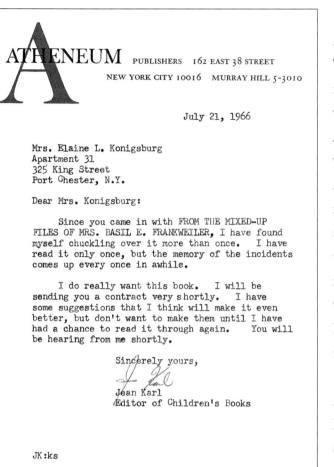

ATHENEUM PUBLISHERS 162 EAST 38 STREET
NEW YORK CITY 10016 MURRAY HILL 5-3010

July 21, 1966

Mrs. Elaine L. Konigsburg
Apartment 31
325 King Street
Port Chester, N.Y.

Dear Mrs. Konigsburg:

Since you came in with FROM THE MIXED-UP
FILES OF MRS. BASIL E. FRANKWEILER, I have found
myself chuckling over it more than once. I have
read it only once, but the memory of the incidents
comes up every once in awhile.

I do really want this book. I will be
sending you a contract very shortly. I have
some suggestions that I think will make it even
better, but don't want to make them until I have
had a chance to read it through again. You will
be hearing from me shortly.

Sincerely yours,

Jean Karl
Editor of Children's Books

JK:ks

Editor Jean Karl's acceptance
letter for *From the Mixed-Up
Files of Mrs. Basil E. Frankweiler*

*Why have you often written
historical fiction?*
Those books have always started with an
interest in art and with the people involved
with that art. *A Proud Taste for Scarlet and
Miniver* (1979), for instance, grew out of my
visits with my children to the Cloisters, the
Metropolitan Museum's collection of
medieval art. I started wondering in particular
about Eleanor of Aquitaine, who was wife to
two kings and mother of two, and who struck
me as essentially a liberated woman at a time
when women were considered chattel. And so
I wrote about her; her times were a water-
shed, and she was magnificent.

Do you have a daily work routine?
I get up, get dressed, and I come to work. Work
expands to fill the time available. That's especially true of housework. So in order to have
time to write when my children were young
and going to school, I had to train myself not to make a bed or wash
a dish until after they had come home from school at lunchtime. I am
training myself now not to answer the mail until the afternoon. I am
having serious talks about this with myself!

Do you have a special place to work?
Oh, yes! I used to work in a converted bedroom at home. Now I have
a marvelous studio behind our house where I can write and do art-
work. [She designed the chair shown on page 49.] When I look out in
one direction from my studio I see a marsh, and if I swivel my chair
around, I see the Atlantic Ocean. I can't believe I'm here.

Do you know from the start how a book will end?
Yes. First, I know my characters. I also know an important incident

that will come in the middle. As I write, my characters take me up to that incident, then past it, right up to the ending foretold.

How do you get to know your characters?

I begin writing. As I continue, I fall in love with some characters and not with others. In *Jennifer, Hecate, Macbeth, William McKinley, and Me, Elizabeth,* for instance, I based the little girl who is called Cynthia on a girl I really didn't like who lived in the apartment house where we lived when I wrote that book. I started out not liking Cynthia—and I didn't like her when I finished the book, either!

Why, by the way, do some of your books, including
Jennifer, Hecate, Macbeth, William McKinley, and Me, Elizabeth,
have such very long titles?

When I finished *Jennifer, Hecate . . .* I didn't have a title for it. I thought, *If I were to ask my oldest child Paul what it was about, he would say, "Oh, it's about a girl and a witch and a toad . . ."* So I put all those names together in what I thought was a rhythmical pattern. It's been my experience that kids just love saying the names.

Why do you sign your books "E. L."
rather than "Elaine" Konigsburg?

When I began writing in the mid-1960s, I thought it was not important for readers to know whether I was male or female. Also, I was a great admirer of E. B. White, so I may have thought that it would bring me luck to submit my first manuscript as "E. L." But if I were starting out today, I would use my first name.

Do you revise much?

Sometimes yes and sometimes no. You have to do justice to your work. I wouldn't want to hand in a sloppy manuscript.

I write the book and then I go back in. Sometimes, I blank out whole pages and redo them; other times, I dab here and I dab there, in just the same way that, as an oil painter, I paint over a spot, let it dry . . . touch it up . . . let it dry . . . until it is right.

Do you, like the title character in
From the Mixed-Up Files of Mrs. Basil E. Frankweiler,
have files of research materials?

I do. I'll clip an article when it first catches my interest, and file it away. I have a file called "Strange," another called "Political Correctness," and another called "Baseball and Jewish." I have a file on Barbara McClintock, a Nobel Prize-winning geneticist I'm fascinated by. I have files on each of my children.

When I was starting work on the book that became *The View from Saturday* (1996), I had the character of Ethan clearly in mind. I had the image of him boarding the school bus, and of Julian entering the bus. I knew that Julian would say that his father was going to make over an old farmhouse as a bed-and-breakfast inn or "B and B." And that's when I took a walk along the beach and remembered that I had in my files a short story called "The B & B Letter." As I walked on I remembered two other stories in my files, and realized that they were

A photograph (left) of two of Konigsburg's three children in the Egyptian wing of the Metropolitan Museum of Art. The snapshot was the basis for the illustration (right) from *From the Mixed-Up Files of Mrs. Basil E. Frankweiler.*

all connected by the same theme even though they had been written over a period of years.

Do you do other kinds of research?

When I was writing *From the Mixed-Up Files* I went with my children to the Metropolitan Museum of Art. They posed, and I took Polaroids of them as Claudia and Jamie. We went all through the museum and ate at the restaurant. We also visited a bus yard in Connecticut.

How do you know when a book is done?

There are two ways. It's partly a matter of instinctive knowledge: I just know. But it's also when my characters have completed their journey, when I've taken my people where I knew they were going.

What do you tell children who want to write?

I always tell them to finish. I tell them that a great many people have talent, but that the difference between being a person of talent and being a writer is the ability to apply the seat of your pants to the seat of your chair, and finish.

I once had the chance to look at the first draft of E. B. White's *Charlotte's Web*, a book I love. I was already an author then and was having trouble with the book I was writing. It was wonderful for me to see that *Charlotte's Web* didn't happen all at once, either. E. B. White had to work at it.

What is the best part of being a writer?

This answer may sound a little rehearsed, and in a sense it is because I have thought about it a lot. Here goes: W. H. Auden has said, "Rite is the link between the dead and the unborn." I believe that reading is a rite as well as a right, and books are the link that can be shared without your having to be there. For example, one of the things on my lifetime checklist of things I wanted to do before I die is see Baryshnikov dance, and I did get to see him dance. But I can never share that experience with my grandchildren. You had to be there. But with books you can share the experience. And from the mail that I get, I know that my books are a link—teacher to student; parent to child; friend to friend; country to country. Being a link between generations and across borders is the best part of a lot of very good parts, all of which are immeasurable—even in fractions, and it sure beats breaking glass in an organic chemistry lab.

An E. L. KONIGSBURG Reader

About the B'nai Bagels, illustrated by the author (Atheneum, 1969; Dell, 1985)

Altogether, One at a Time, illustrated by Gail E. Haley and others (Atheneum, 1971; Aladdin, 1975)

From the Mixed-Up Files of Mrs. Basil E. Frankweiler, illustrated by the author (Atheneum, 1967; Aladdin, 1972)

Jennifer, Hecate, Macbeth, William McKinley, and Me, Elizabeth, illustrated by the author (Atheneum, 1967; Dell, 1984)

A Proud Taste for Scarlet and Miniver, illustrated by the author (Atheneum, 1979; Dell, 1985)

The Second Mrs. Giaconda (Atheneum, 1975; Aladdin, 1981)

T-Backs, T-Shirts, Coat, and Suit (Atheneum, 1993; Hyperion, 1995)

Throwing Shadows (Atheneum, 1979; Aladdin, 1981)

Up from Jericho Tel (Atheneum, 1986; Aladdin, 1998)

The View from Saturday (Atheneum, 1996; Aladdin, 1998)

LOIS LOWRY

(BORN MARCH 20, 1937, HONOLULU, HAWAII)

As a child, Lois Lowry had many homes. Her family moved—from Honolulu to New York to Tokyo and back to New York—each time her father, a career officer in the United States military, was restationed. When Lowry's father left for service in the Pacific during World War II, her mother took Lois and her older sister, Helen, to Pennsylvania to live with the girls' grandparents until the end of the war. The quiet enjoyment Lowry found in reading and writing throughout her childhood years served as comforting constants against this shifting backdrop of home surroundings, schools, and friends.

Lowry married young and soon had four children of her own. Her busy new life forced her to postpone thoughts of a writing career until her mid-thirties. Her father was a skilled photographer. She became one, too, and when Lowry finally did begin to write professionally, she realized that writing and photography were in many ways alike. Words could evoke sharp, clear pictures of a character or scene. The writer's voice was like the camera angle chosen for a picture. Lowry

found that she could capture the humorous angle of her characters' predicaments, as in the Anastasia Krupnik novels. Or the focus could instead fall on her characters' more serious concerns, as in *The Giver* (1993). But whether being funny or serious, Lowry has always tried, she says, to encourage her readers to form their own way of viewing the world, and to answer for themselves "their own questions about life, identity, and human relationships."

What kind of girl were you?

Allow me to digress—because that is how I think. I received an E-mail not long ago from someone I had not heard from since the eighth grade. She had seen a video that my publisher made about me. Her message read, "There you were. The same outgoing, confident person that you were when you were twelve years old." My mouth dropped because *my* memory is that when I was twelve years old I was the least eloquent person I knew—mute and self-conscious and awkward. It's funny, isn't it, how other people's impressions of oneself can be so very different from one's own. But one thing that I think other people would agree on about me is that, like my character Anastasia Krupnik, I made my way through those awkward years by having a sense of humor.

Lois, age 10

Did you enjoy reading as a child?

With help from my sister Helen, who was three years older, I learned to read at the age of three. From then on, I read voraciously.

Did you have favorite books?

Yes, and I'm still looking for the boy named Allen Stewart who lived across the street from me in Bay Ridge, Brooklyn, because he borrowed my copy of *Mr. Popper's Penguins* in 1941 and never returned it! I also loved *Mary Poppins* and Nancy Drew.

My mother, who'd taught kindergarten before she married, continued to read to us long after I had begun reading on my own. I was eight or nine when she read us Marjorie Kinnan Rawlings's *The Yearling*, which was a landmark in my life as a reader and writer: It was while listening to that novel that I realized that the words of a book could stir intense emotions.

When did you decide you wanted to be a writer?

By third or fourth grade. The public school I attended paid no special attention to creativity, so writing was something I did privately. I filled up notebooks at home with stories and poems. A favorite great-aunt who lived in town and a retired judge who was a friend of my grandfather's both took a literary interest in me. I showed them my writing. They encouraged me and gave me books.

Do you recall the first time you saw your name in print?

Yes: August 1947, to be precise. One does remember these things, even though the experience proved to be a mixed blessing. I was ten years old, and my parents had given me a subscription to a children's magazine that published letters from readers. I sent in many letters. Finally, while I was away at camp that summer, I heard from home that my latest letter, in which I had described my family, was going to be published. I was excited but also scared. The problem was, I had told a lie to the camp counselors, whom I had noticed paid more attention to campers with college-aged brothers. I'd told my counselor that I had a brother at Princeton, which wasn't true, and that he might visit me. But in the letter that was about to be published, I had described my *real* family. When a copy of the magazine arrived, instead of proudly showing it to everyone, I hid it in the trunk under my bed for fear of being found out.

Lois, in Japan at age 12, wearing a traditional Japanese kimono

Was there a moment when you realized you were no longer a child?

I think life consists of a series of moments that are important realizations. In *Autumn Street* (1980), which in many ways is an autobiographical novel, I describe one such moment, when the narrator, who is me, recalls lying awake in bed one night as a young girl, thinking about her sister: "Suddenly I realized her dreams would always be different from mine." All children have that moment—whether they remember it or not—when they become aware of themselves as individuals, different from everyone else.

Another such moment came for me a few years later. I liked being a child, and around my eleventh birthday I found myself, with some sadness, thinking, *I'm moving into the time of eleven, the time of being old.*

Paradoxically, as an adult in my twenties, I felt very young again. I had dropped out of college at nineteen, gotten married, and had four children before I was twenty-five. I felt *too* young to have so many adult responsibilities. And I realized then that I would have to postpone my writing career for years.

When did you finally begin to write professionally?

> **I realized that the words of a book could stir intense emotions.**

Years later, when my youngest child was in high school. I began as a journalist. Because I had studied photography, I took my own photographs, too. For a time I also did photographic portraits of children. The photo on the jacket of *Number the Stars* (1989) is one of those early portraits. The photo on the cover of *The Giver* is a portrait I took of an artist about whom I had written an article.

When I was writing for magazines, I also wrote fiction. In 1975, a children's book editor read a short story I had published in *Redbook* and wrote to me to ask if I would consider writing a book for kids. It was because of that request that I wrote my first novel, *A Summer to Die (1977)*.

Do you have a daily work routine?

My house once belonged to a doctor who worked at home. His office is now mine. His waiting room is my dining room! My routine is pretty casual. I sit at my computer every day, but I fool around a lot. Friends know that I'm usually available for a Thursday afternoon movie. Yet I know that even as I am fooling around, I am thinking. A lot of preliminary work takes place in my head—when I'm driving home from the movies, for example. I can picture a book in my head early on as if it were a photograph or film. For that reason, once I start the actual writing it can go very quickly. I'll work for several hours each day. It may take two months to work my way through to the ending. Then comes the time for revision. I revised *The Giver* twice quite thoroughly. The Anastasia books, on the other hand, are more straightforward and don't require much revision.

How did you change The Giver*?*

Several editors read the first manuscript and found some things puzzling, so in the rewriting process I tried to make things clearer without sacrificing the magical, mysterious quality of the book. One of the things that was added during the revision was the character of Rosemary. She hadn't existed in the first version.

Do you know from the start how a book is going to end?

I usually know the beginning and the ending, but not the middle until I sit down and write it. There are surprises along the way. For instance, in *Rabble Starkey* (1987), a character named Norman started out in my mind as a very minor character—just an obnoxious brat. But midway through the writing, another side to him began to emerge. I realized that he behaved the way he did in part because he was an adolescent going through the throes of growing up that all kids his age experience. And so he became a more rounded, more interesting character.

Do you do research for some of your books?

I dedicated *Number the Stars* to Annelise Platt, a Danish-born woman who became my friend years ago when we were both living in Maine. She made me aware of the history of Denmark during World War II. It was from her that I got the idea to write *Number the Stars* and that I learned many of the details that went into it.

An old photograph has the power to trigger a whole set of memories and emotions.

I also read about that period and looked at old photographs. A myth developed that the Christian citizens of Denmark, including the king, wore yellow stars on their clothing as a sign of solidarity with the Jews. I wanted that to be true, because it is such a wonderful image. I did not mention it in my book, however, because through my research I found that in fact it did not happen.

What was it like going through your own family's photographs while writing Looking Back (1998)?

After my son, who was in the air force, died in a plane crash in 1995, I put together a little book of family photos for his daughter, who was then just a year and a half old, for her to remember him by. As I looked at more and more family photographs, including those from my own childhood, I began to notice, for the first time, correlations

Lowry, with granddaughter
Nadine

between scenes captured in some of the old pictures and certain scenes in my books. I was fascinated to discover those connections and to realize that an old photograph had the power to trigger a whole set of memories and emotions.

How do you know when a book is done?
It's harder to determine now than it was fifteen years ago. I'm not a good typist, and back when I typed my manuscripts I sometimes did less revision than I would have liked. Now, with computers, revising is so easy. It's so much fun to change—and change—things. I could go on forever. I have to make myself quit.

What do you tell kids who want to write?
I wish them well. I feel a sense of kinship with them. I say that the way one learns to write is by reading—and developing a passion for language used in meaningful ways. Thoughts of publication are for later, for grown-up writers who have to earn a living.

What is the best thing about being a writer?
The writing itself. The fact that I can sit at my desk, play with language, and make a living at it just astounds me.

A LOIS LOWRY Reader

All About Sam, illustrated by Diane deGroat (Houghton Mifflin, 1988; Dell, 1989)

Anastasia Krupnik, illustrated by Diane deGroat (Houghton Mifflin, 1979; Dell, 1984)

Autumn Street (Houghton Mifflin, 1980; Dell, 1986)

Find a Stranger, Say Good-Bye (Houghton Mifflin, 1978; Dell, 1990)

The Giver (Houghton Mifflin, 1993; Dell, 1994)

Looking Back: A Book of Memories (Houghton Mifflin, 1998; Dell, 2000)

Number the Stars (Houghton Mifflin, 1989; Dell, 1990)

Rabble Starkey (Houghton Mifflin, 1987; Dell, 1988)

Stay! Keeper's Story, illustrated by True Kelley (Houghton Mifflin, 1997; Dell, 1999)

Taking Care of Terrific (Houghton Mifflin, 1983; Dell, 1984)

ANN M. MARTIN

(BORN AUGUST 12, 1955, PRINCETON, NEW JERSEY)

Creativity—and a vibrant sense of fun—played a big part in Ann M. Martin's secure childhood. Martin's mother was a preschool teacher and her father was an artist whose drawings appeared regularly in *The New Yorker*. Both parents encouraged their older daughter's love of fantasy and her talent for making things. Both were more amused than surprised when, having arrived once at an airport hours too early for their flight, young Ann found a laminating machine and proceeded to laminate everything in her wallet.

Martin spent her first year after college teaching autistic children. She then took a job with a publishing company and, a few years later, in 1983, published her first three children's books, including one coauthored by Betsy Ryan called *My Puppy Scrapbook*, with illustrations by her father, Henry Martin.

The first Baby-sitters Club books—numbers 1 through 4—were published three years later, in August 1986. No one knew at first how popular Martin's "little miniseries" would be. Readers quickly found the books, however, and must have told their friends about them; soon Martin's editor wanted two more stories for the series. When number 6—*Kristy's Big Day*—became a bestseller, the author shifted into high gear, for a time writing one or more new volumes every month.

One of the most prolific—and widely read—authors ever to write for children, Martin has amazingly clear and detailed memories of her childhood. She still recalls exactly how she felt on her first day of school, on her tenth birthday, and at her senior prom. As a fiction writer, Martin says, she has a chance to revisit these early experiences. And she can make them turn out any way she wants.

What kind of child were you?

Very shy. I loved arts and crafts and learned how to sew and do needlework when I was very little. I liked writing, though I had no idea of becoming a writer. I thought I would become a teacher like my mother.

Ann, age 9, in her first horse show

Did you like to read?

I was a huge reader. I loved *The Story of Babar*, *Mary Poppins*, *The Wonderful Wizard of Oz*, and the Doctor Doolittle books. I read *Harriet the Spy* just before our family took a long train trip across the western United States. I spent most of the trip taking notes on the other passengers. I liked to make up my own fantasies. My younger sister and I were always off in the woods with our dolls, making little habitats in the tree roots for them, creating our own worlds.

My father, who was a cartoonist, encouraged this. He was always drawing for us and taking us to the circus and to magic shows. I loved the circus: waiting for the spotlight to come on at the center of the ring, for the ringmaster to appear, seeing people do all those things that you'd never see people do in real life. I loved even the plate-spinners!

> *My sister and I were always off in the woods with our dolls, creating our own worlds for them.*

What else did you like to do as a child?

> I played endless games of Life and Clue.

Did you like school?

> I enjoyed schoolwork but I hated speaking in class and giving reports. Gym class was another big stumbling block! I hated Spud and once even asked my mother to write a note to get me out of playing it. I hated being onstage, too. For that reason, Mary Anne, in the Baby-sitters Club series, and Sara, the heroine of my novel *Stage Fright* (1984), are the characters from my books who are most like the girl I was.

Is Mary Anne your favorite Baby-sitters Club character?

> Actually, Kristy is. Kristy—and Karen from the Little Sister series—are both very outspoken and have lots of ideas. They are a lot like my own best friend, Beth, from when I was growing up. Kristy was also the first character I created for the Baby-sitters Club. She's the one who thinks of the club. The very first book in the series is about her. I like her for all those reasons, too.

Were you ever a baby-sitter yourself?

> I was a mother's helper at ten and began baby-sitting more seriously when I was thirteen. Nothing very wild ever happened to me, but baby-sitting was my main source of money until I got to college.

What did you do with the money you earned?

> I saved it for something special. When I was fifteen, I used my savings to buy the thing I wanted most of all—a sewing machine. In high school I made a lot of my own clothes. Now I sew for my godchildren and for my friends' kids.

Did you like to baby-sit for other reasons, too?

> I think the reason that older kids want to baby-sit is the same reason that younger kids, especially, want pets: It's the idea of becoming responsible for another living being, having always been the one that other people were responsible for.

Did you have pets as a child?

I've always had cats. When I was in the second grade, I belonged to something called the Kit-Kat Klub—but I can't remember what the club actually did.

I have three cats now: Willy, Woody, and Guss. I like that cats are both totally independent and very affectionate. Mine are real snugglers, and I honestly think they have senses of humor and that they consider themselves quite funny!

When did you decide to become a writer?

Not until I was in college. By then, several teachers had told me that I wrote well. But I didn't see writing as a career option. For a long time, I think I thought all writers were dead!

How did you go about getting started as a writer?

After college, I taught for a year at a school for children with special needs. Then I worked as an editor of children's books for a number of years. I don't know why, but as an editor, and then as a writer, I found myself gravitating toward books for middle-grade kids.

What is a typical workday like for you?

I'm an early riser. I get up at five-thirty or so, settle down at my desk by eight, check my E-mail, and write all morning. That's when I feel freshest. In the afternoon I may read, edit galleys, go to a meeting, or answer my mail.

Martin, at her desk

Where do you get your ideas for books?

From childhood memories, things I've read about in the paper, and sometimes pure fantasy. I start with an idea and then write out a series of increasingly detailed outlines of the story. That way I always have a road map as I write.

Do you do research for some of your books?

If a story is going to cover a medical topic, or a specific problem such as a learning disability or anorexia, research is essential. My editor and I will also have the manuscript read by a doctor or other expert to make sure that everything in the story is accurate.

How do you know when a book is finished?

Because I outline my books in advance, I usually can tell when I have tied up all the loose ends. Even so, it's sometimes hard to write the very last sentence. It's the last thing the reader will read and it has to be just right.

What have you learned from the many thousands of letters kids write to you about the Baby-sitters Club books?

> *I start with an idea and then write out a series of increasingly detailed outlines of the story.*

When the Baby-sitters Club series was just getting started, there were certain subjects that I thought might be a bit too weighty for my readers. I wrote a couple of early books about the death of a grandparent and a pet. But I thought that I probably wasn't going to write about child abuse or substance abuse or the death of a peer or a parent. After the series had been out for quite a few years, however, I received a whole slew of letters from kids who wanted to read a book about the death of a friend. They had had that experience themselves, and so I wrote *Mary Anne and the Memory Garden* (number 93, 1996), which tells about the death of Amelia Freeman in a car crash, and how her friends mourned for her.

What do you tell kids who want to write?

To read a lot and read widely. By reading a lot, you learn to recognize the difference between good writing and bad writing. By reading widely—journalism, poetry, fiction, nonfiction—you find out what kinds of writing interest you the most.

Keeping a journal or diary is good writing experience. A journal also can become a good source of writing ideas. It's important not to force yourself to write in a journal every day, though. I kept a journal—very sporadically—when I was growing up. Even now, I like to reread it to see what I was thinking about then.

What do you like to do when you're not writing?

I still love to sew and do needlework. It's almost as important to me as writing. I love having fabric in my hands, the feel of it, and working with colors and textures.

What is the best part of being a writer for you?

Writing can be hard work but mostly it feels exciting, especially when I'm very involved with the characters or the scene. I can feel the excitement in my stomach. It's almost like being at the circus.

An ANN M. MARTIN Reader

The Baby-sitters Club series (Scholastic, 1986–)

The Baby-sitters' Little Sister series, illustrated by Susan Crocca Tang

(Scholastic, 1988–)

The **California Diaries** series (Scholastic, 1997–)

Leo the Magnicat, illustrated by Emily Arnold McCully (Scholastic, 1996)

My Puppy Scrapbook

(coauthored by Betsy Ryan, illustrated by Henry Martin; Scholastic, 1983)

P.S. Longer Letter Later

(coauthored by Paula Danziger; Scholastic, 1998; Scholastic, 1999)

Stage Fright, illustrated by Blanche Sims (Holiday House, 1984; Scholastic, 1990)

Ten Kids, No Pets (Holiday House, 1988; Scholastic, 1990)

With You and Without You (Holiday House, 1986; Scholastic, 1990)

NICHOLASA MOHR

(BORN NOVEMBER 1, 1938, NEW YORK, NEW YORK)

"The creative mind," Nicholasa Mohr has said, "is a powerful instrument, and I believe we are all born with this gift." Growing up as a Puerto Rican child in New York City, Mohr quickly learned what it was like to be treated as a second-class citizen. And she learned to rely on her own imagination both as a survival tool and a source of joy.

As a schoolgirl, Mohr read widely and became skilled at drawing. She dreamed of becoming an artist, even after a junior high guidance counselor refused to recommend her for a high school that would have allowed her to specialize in fine art. As a young person from a poor family like hers, she was told, she should instead learn a useful trade such as dressmaking.

After high school, Mohr nonetheless managed to study art and to set out on a career as a printmaker and painter. In the early 1970s, a publisher who knew that little had been written about the lives of Puerto Ricans suggested to Mohr that she consider writing about her childhood experiences. She decided to try, and the work she began then grew into her first book, a novel for young adults called *Nilda* (1973). Mohr illustrated *Nilda* herself. With time, writing became more important to her and finally traded places with art as the major creative work through which she continues "to search and to learn."

What kind of child were you?

Perky. Into everything. My mother didn't know what to do with me. Because I had six older brothers and a male cousin all living at home, in our Bronx apartment, I knew early on how to maneuver and how to take care of myself. I knew how to take a punch! I was also good at hopscotch and jump rope. Very athletic.

Nicholasa, at age 6

Did you grow up bilingual?

Yes. My brothers spoke English with me at home. We played—and fought!—in English. But with my mother I spoke in the sweet sounds of Puerto Rican Spanish, and because of this, Spanish has always felt like a safety net to me. It is the language I associate with my first experiences of being loved and hugged. Growing up, it was the language of my community.

Did you like to read as a child?

Oh, yes. By the time I was four, and with the help of my brothers, I taught myself to read and write English. I learned on comic books such as *Dick Tracy* and *Popeye*. We were a working-class family and didn't have a lot of books at home, and so when I first began reading

I went around the apartment attempting to read the labels on all our cans of beans and cereal boxes. It was just thrilling. By the time I was seven, I was writing notes in English for my mother, who was barely literate in Spanish and completely illiterate in English.

Did you go to the public library?

The library was where I spent my life! It was quiet there, especially for someone like me who lived in such a crowded apartment. Many librarians befriended me. There, I could read whatever I wanted. It was a wonderful place to be.

Do you remember the first book you ever checked out?

It was *Pinocchio*. I took it out seven times. Finally, the librarian said to me, "You know, it will *always* be here." As a teenager, when my mother died I went to live with an aunt. At that time I worked part-time in the library as a page girl to earn some money.

Did you enjoy school?

I was aware early on that often when I went to school I was going into hostile territory.

School was not always a pleasant experience for me. For example, I was eager to learn and was an excellent student in English. Nonetheless I was aware early on that often when I went to school I was going into hostile territory. The library, on the other hand, was an exception, but not the public schools.

My first day of kindergarten was an unfortunate experience. I had already taught myself how to count as well as to read and write, and when I tried to show my teacher what I could do, she would have none of it. "Look at this show-off," she said, scolding me for knowing too much. Later that same year some new girls arrived from Puerto Rico who spoke Spanish very well but knew no English. When I tried to help out by explaining to them in Spanish what the teacher was saying, she became furious. "This is not your country," she said. "You speak English here." For the rest of the year I got that kind of treatment.

In junior high school I opted to take the Spanish class, but my teacher, who had a thick Irish-American Bronx accent, insisted that we speak Castilian Spanish—as it is spoken in Spain, with a European

Illustration by Mohr, from *Nilda*

accent—rather than speak with a Caribbean Spanish accent. It was like asking an American-born English speaker to talk like an English citizen. It felt like play-acting, and all of us Puerto Rican children and other Latino children would laugh. But finally it became stressful and humiliating, and I decided to study French instead. I wrote about this experience in my novel *Nilda*.

Things got a little better in the fifties, when Puerto Ricans came to live in New York City by the tens of thousands. I felt less isolated and always had a group of buddies to hang out with. I also described some of these experiences in my collection of stories *El Bronx Remembered* (1975).

Besides reading, what else did you like to do as a girl?
I loved to draw. I was a very good artist. I would draw people, furniture, my fantasies—in fact, whatever came into my mind. Drawing also helped me.

My art gave me an edge, a distinction, as it does for the young heroine of *Going Home* (1986). I once overheard a teacher, who did not especially like me, say, "That Nicholasa can't be *all* bad. She can draw." And I could persuade the local tough kids out of beating me up by offering to draw their portraits. I would make sure they looked really good, almost like movie stars!

You became a professional artist, then turned to writing. Was it hard to make the change?

To my own astonishment, no. For one thing, I was always a voracious reader and so I had quite a lot of wonderful authors and books as prime examples. And as an artist, I had been working for years in that special place where creativity is a part of your life. So for me it was a matter of going from one craft to another and bringing along all the skills that I had worked hard to gather and perfect.

A scene from the 1999
Henry Street Settlement
Urban Youth Theater
production of
El Bronx Remembered

Why did you make that change?

One reason is that I knew that not everyone could afford to collect art. I liked the idea that almost anybody could afford to buy a book—or could go to the library and get it for free.

What is a typical workday like for you?

I get up, have breakfast, check my E-mail, and by ten o'clock am at my computer. I try to put in as much as four hours each day. Then I may go over what I wrote earlier or take care of other work that needs to get done, or go to the gym or for a walk. When I'm writing, I like it to be absolutely quiet, and I don't like interruptions.

What is it like to work with an editor?

Sometimes I might get too close to my work and think, *That's the most wonderful scene I've ever written*—when really I should delete that whole scene. A good editor will come along and explain to me why I should omit or add relevant material.

A good editor will ask the right questions. She or he may help me realize that a character is weak or that a section needs to be extended or moved from the middle, to the beginning or the end.

Do you revise your work much?

That depends. A writer has to be willing to accept that there may be

> **I had been working for years in that special place where creativity is a part of your life.**

times when he or she may have to write entire chapters or sections over and over again. There's one short story in my book for adults, *A Matter of Pride and Other Stories* (1997), that needed so much rewriting, it took five years to finish. At other times a writer is blessed, and the story pours out without much need for rewriting. Kids need to remember that rewriting is nothing to feel ashamed about. It simply means that you are dedicated to getting it as perfect as possible. It's the same as for an athlete who has to learn how to make that basket or get that ball over the net. No time spent writing is ever really wasted, because you are always honing your skills.

How do you know when a story or a book is done?

I just know, and that is probably because I've done it so often.

What is the best part about being a writer?

Having the chance to write about things that are important to me. Events that I know well, heartfelt things. And, having the opportunity to tell good stories.

A NICHOLASA MOHR Reader

El Bronx Remembered (Harper, 1975; Bantam, 1976)

Felita, illustrated by Ray Cruz (Dial, 1979; Bantam, 1990)

Going Home (Dial, 1986; Bantam, 1989)

Growing Up in the Sanctuary of My Imagination: A Memoir (Messner, 1994)

In Nueva New York (Dial, 1977; Dell, 1979)

The Magic Shell/El Regalo Mágico, illustrated by Rudy Gutierrez

(English and Spanish language editions: Scholastic, 1995; Scholastic, 1998)

A Matter of Pride and Other Stories (Arte Publico, 1997)

Nilda, illustrated by the author (Harper, 1973; Bantam, 1974)

The Song of El Coquí and Other Tales of Puerto Rico/La Canción del Coquí y otros cuentos de Puerto Rico, retold and coillustrated with Antonio Martorell

(English and Spanish language editions: Viking, 1995)

*

GARY PAULSEN

(BORN MAY 17, 1939, MINNEAPOLIS, MINNESOTA)

Gary Paulsen first learned survival skills as a child growing up in a deeply troubled home. Paulsen's hard-drinking, often absent parents could not be counted on for basic love and attention. By the age of twelve, the future author of *Hatchet* (1987) had taught himself to keep house, make his own fun, and live for weeks at a time in the wilderness. Dogs were his most faithful friends during those early years. They taught him respect for the "ancient and . . . beautiful bond" between humans and nature.

Paulsen traveled a long and winding path on his way to becoming a writer. Asked once to name the careers he has had over the years, Paulsen wrote: "teacher, field engineer, editor, soldier, actor, director, farmer, rancher, truck driver, trapper, professional archer, migrant farm worker, singer, and sailor." The list reads like one of his own adventure stories. He was twenty-seven when he published his first book, *The Special War* (1966), an adult book about Vietnam. He found his true audience a few years later when he realized that "art reaches out to newness. . . . Adults aren't new. . . . Young people know the score."

Gary, at age 4

What kind of child were you?

I had a really rough childhood. Both my parents were drunks and just hated each other. They fought and screamed and never should have been married. I can remember hiding under the kitchen table one day and just wishing they were gone. So to me childhood was mainly something to get through alive. Now, though, I'm actually grateful for some of those early experiences.

Grateful in what way?

Because I was pretty much on my own by the age of seven or eight, I learned about tenacity and independence and the willingness to fight. And I can go back now to some of the things that happened to me and write about them. They're like a mine that I can harvest.

How did you survive?

At one time, when we were living in an apartment in a small Minnesota town, I moved down into the basement of our building by myself. My parents were so drunk, they didn't know the difference. I had found a place in back of the furnace, a sort of alcove, with a half-sized couch and a light hanging from the ceiling. That became my home. I'd usually take down a quart of milk and would eat grape jelly and peanut butter sandwiches down there. I made a lot of airplane models. And I slept there at night. Or I would take off for a week and go stay with an uncle to work on his farm or to go hunting. Half the time my parents wouldn't know I was gone.

Did you enjoy spending time alone in the woods, as so many of your characters do?

I fostered myself to the woods. Whenever I went into the woods, all the hassles of life were very quickly forgotten. It's still that way for me. Sailing's the same.

Paulsen, relaxing on the deck
of his sailboat, *Felicity*

Were there any adults who cared about you then?

My grandmother was wonderful. She told me stories and was my
mother figure. *The Cookcamp* (1991) is virtually nonfiction. The work-
men I wrote about in that book would take me for rides in their trucks.
They sort of adopted me. I still remember their enormous hands that
were big enough to cover a stove lid.

There were also my uncles and aunts, who were all Scandinavian.
Although they didn't think of themselves as storytellers, they would sit
and talk, and tell about their youth and about things they had seen. I
loved listening to them, and what they told *were* stories, beautiful stories.

Do you have childhood memories of World War II?

My father was an army officer in Europe during the war. I would go to
the movies with my mother and see the latest newsreels with footage
from the battlefront, and look for my father in them.

What kind of student were you?

A miserable one! I flunked ninth grade and barely got through high school. I did have one high school history teacher, though, Mr. Carlson, who made history come alive for me. He was just grand.

Did you like to read?

For a long time I was a poor reader, too. When I was thirteen or fourteen, I sold newspapers in bars at night. I found that if I waited for the drunks to get a little cranked up, I could hustle them for more money— instead of a dime, I'd get a quarter for a paper. This was in Minnesota, where it can get really cold. So one night when it was thirty below, I went into the library to warm myself up while I was waiting. The librarian, who had seen me come in, asked if she could help me. "No," I said, "I just want to get warm." "Would you like a library card?" It was a very small town and I'm sure she knew exactly who I was and all about my parents. I answered, "Yeh," in a smart-alecky way. So she gave me a card, with my name on it, and—God!—it was astonishing what happened to me. It was as though I suddenly had an identity: I was a person. "You want a book?" she asked. "Yeh," I said, still smart-alecky. I don't remember what book she chose for me, but I took the thing home and read it in the basement of that grubby apartment building. It took me a month. Over the next two years, she and I became friends. Eventually, I was reading two or three books a week. I owe her everything I've become.

> *I loved listening to them, and what they told were stories, beautiful stories.*

When did you decide to become a writer?

Not until years later. I don't know why, but one night when I was about twenty-seven and had a job working for an aerospace company at a tracking station, it just came to me that I wanted to write. I had never thought of writing before then. I didn't even know what a manuscript was. But it was an absolute dead-bang certainty. So I went to Hollywood and took a job working for a company that published magazines. They did everything—farmer's journals, paint magazines, motorcycle magazines. Once I edited a coffin magazine. It was very good training. Editing taught me to get to the point with words. And it taught me that writing isn't about ego but about getting the words right.

The view from Paulsen's sled in the Iditarod

Do you have a daily work routine?

I can write anywhere. On airplanes, boats. In motels. I have a laptop that I take with me on trips. Since running the Iditarod, a 1,049 mile dogsled race from Nome to Anchorage, Alaska, I've been able to write eighteen hours a day.

What was the Iditarod like?

It's an incredible experience. It changes you forever about all things, kind of like combat does. It affects how you work and how you think. You enter a state of primitive exaltation. For one thing, it's stunningly beautiful. And I don't think anyone who has run the race is ever normal again. You no longer fit. For instance, after I came back from my first race, someone told me about bicycling. I said, "That sounds like fun." *My* first bicycle trip was eight hundred miles long. It seemed easy to me. I didn't have to feed the bike or wipe its feet. I'd stop at night and stay in a motel instead of sleep on the ground next to the dogs. It never occurred to me that I couldn't do it. So the Iditarod taught me not to put limits on myself, and it made it harder for me to be around most people. That's what *Brian's Return* (1999), the second sequel to *Hatchet,* is about. Brian can't be with people anymore, so he goes back to the woods.

> *Editing taught me that writing isn't about ego but about getting the words right.*

The Iditarod also caused me to give up hunting. As I was training for my first race, I realized I couldn't kill a dog. My sled dogs had become like people to me. And if I couldn't kill a dog, I couldn't trap coyotes anymore, because they're dogs. And if I couldn't trap coyotes, I couldn't trap beaver because they're neat animals, too. They think, have homes and families.

Do you have any dogs now?

Two Border collies, one terrier, and three Chihuahuas. I go to the pound and say, "Give me the next one you're going to whack." I don't ask what it is. The dog I take home just got lucky. Dogs have been good to me, and I love them.

You have written so much.
Do you work on only one book at a time?

As I write one, I might be researching one or two others. *Nightjohn* (1993), for instance, took years of historical research. I wrote many other books during that time.

How do you get your ideas?

I don't know why, but if I'm working on a book, it will cause ideas for two more. I've currently got 130 ideas for books. I'll never catch up.

How do you know when a book is finished?

In a way, I don't know. I'll pull a book up on the computer and start playing with it—rewriting it—even after it's been published.

Do kids write to you?

I get about four hundred letters a day. If there's one recurring theme, it's that nobody's listening to them. I think that's a shame.

What do you tell kids who want to write?

Read. Read *when* they tell you not to read, and read *what* they tell you not to read. Read like a wolf eats! You can't learn anything watching television. It's very important to turn the box off—and carry a book with you all the time.

Is there one place in the world where you feel most at home?

At one time I would have said the North Woods. I love storms and difficulties. And I've always loved the sea. The rhythm of it. The vastness of it. But I don't know that I feel at home there.

What is the best part of being a writer?

The dance with words. In fact, when things are kind of funny and grim, it is the thing that most sustains me. I just love it, I really do.

A GARY PAULSEN Reader

Brian's Return (Delacorte, 1999)

The Cookcamp (Orchard, 1991; Dell, 1992)

Dancing Carl (Bradbury, 1983; Puffin, 1987)

Dogsong (Bradbury, 1985; Aladdin, 1995)

Harris and Me (Harcourt Brace, 1993; Dell, 1995)

Hatchet (Bradbury, 1987; Puffin, 1988)

My Life in Dog Years, illustrated by Ruth Wright Paulsen (Delacorte, 1998; Dell, 1999)

Nightjohn (Doubleday, 1993; Dell, 1995)

Soldier's Heart (Doubleday, 1998; Dell, 2000)

The Transall Saga (Delacorte, 1998; Dell, 1999)

The Winter Room (Orchard, 1989; Dell, 1991)

Woodsong, illustrated by Ruth Wright Paulsen (Bradbury, 1990; Puffin, 1991)

✳

JON SCIESZKA

(BORN SEPTEMBER 8, 1954, FLINT, MICHIGAN)

Jon Scieszka has always had a knack for finding humor in unlikely places—in math, for instance, and in scary old stories like the one about the wolf and the three little pigs. His mother, who was a nurse and a naturally funny person, and his father, who was an elementary school principal, read him Dr. Seuss and later encouraged him to find and follow his own interests. Math and science both fascinated him, but it was literature that brought him to New York following college. John had decided to become a novelist.

Teaching grade school to make a living, Scieszka found that he liked to joke with children and that he enjoyed being around them. He found that he often could remember what school had been like for him—not just the fun parts but also the worry, for instance, that goes with trying to come up with the right answer to teachers' questions. When a student in his math class said one day, "What the heck is x and why don't we just figure it out once and for all and write it down?" he realized that he knew exactly how that child felt.

Scieszka did not make the connection right away between work-

ing with children and writing for them. But once he did, he found that he had many ideas for stories. He met artist Lane Smith after Scieszka's wife, Jeri, and Smith's future wife, Molly Leach, became friends at the office where they both worked as art directors. By then, Scieszka had written but not yet published *The True Story of the Three Little Pigs* (1989). Smith made some drawings to go along with the story. Together they set out in search of a publisher who would not think their book too goofy or strange.

Jon, third-grade photo

What kind of boy were you?

A nice boy, and I always did good! Actually, I was a stealth kid, the kind of guy who sits in the back of the class and cracks jokes. I would get my friends in trouble by making them laugh while I sat by quietly, trying to look innocent.

Did you have brothers and sisters?

I'm the second oldest of six brothers. Jim, the oldest, and I often baby-sat for the little guys. I'd tell stories—and terrorize them! They were a great audience. And if they got out of line, I'd just say we were going to call the Bad Boys' Home to come and get them. Then I'd reach for the phone, and they'd all shout, "No, no! We'll go to bed!"

What did the Scieszkas do for Halloween?

Our family had a few costumes that we took turns wearing. I started out as the Pink Bunny. We all started with *that* one. Then I moved on to the Witch. I tried the Ghost one year, but had trouble with the eye-holes and fell off one too many porches.

Did you like books as a kid?

I loved Dr. Seuss's *Green Eggs and Ham*, P. D. Eastman's *Go, Dog, Go!*, and *The Carrot Seed* by Ruth Krauss and Crockett Johnson. I'd make my mom read them over and over until they were burned into my brain.

Did you enjoy writing?

I was so jazzed by the rhyming in Dr. Seuss's books that I tried to write my own funky little verses. From then on, I always wanted to be a writer. I can remember in fourth and fifth grade looking on the library shelves for the place where books by me would be, in alphabetical order. I always looked in the adult section! There was just one problem: I wasn't sure how to spell Scieszka (pronounced CHESS-kah)!

My teachers couldn't even pronounce my last name. During roll, the teacher would say: "Tom Schmidt. Jon . . ." Then there'd be this big pause. For years, I signed my school papers "Jon S." Even now, late at night, I still can't quite get *all* the letters.

Did you ever want to be anything besides a writer?

> *It got me to look at all sorts of things in surprising ways, and that's great training for a writer.*

For a long time, I don't think I believed that real people actually became writers. Certainly I'd never met an author. So, for a while I wanted to be a forest ranger—a guy who climbed trees all day. But my mother tried to steer me away from tree-climbing. She would say, "You can be a doctor. Make a lot of money and not work really hard." That sounded great. That's a nurse joke. But I liked science, so in college I took both premed courses and literature courses. I'd mix the two together. In science class, I'd write a little poem about the trout skull we were taking apart, and in English class I'd be busy secretly memorizing the circulatory system of the cat. It was a great education because it got me to look at all sorts of things in surprising ways, and that's great training for a writer.

How did you end up writing for children?

I first tried writing grown-up fiction while painting people's apartments to make a living. I then got a job teaching elementary school. That's when I rediscovered kids' books, and kids. Every bad joke I ever learned from my dad I could try out on them, and the little knuckleheads thought it was mine! Like, "I just flew in from Chicago and boy are my arms tired."

What were your classes like?

We were a tight little family. Friday was Joke Day. I'd get a microphone and an amplifier from the AV room. It was great—at first. But then we started hearing a lot of jokes from older brothers and sisters. I still remember the one about the ants on the log. The punch line was something like, "Don't flush, don't flush!" Finally, I had to say, "Okay, kids, we'd better make some rules."

Did the children teach you anything?

Teaching children taught me everything. Teaching them reminded me how often grown-ups ask kids—in math class and English and music or wherever—to go out on a limb, to try something completely new that they might fail at in front of all their friends. It reminded me how scary that can be. When I thought about taking a year off from teaching to try writing full-time, I told myself, "If they can go out on a limb, so can I."

Where do you get your ideas for books?

I used to say, "From a little old lady in Schenectady, who sends me one each week." But the real answer is, from thinking—and from other books. As a kid, I always wondered whether there was a list somewhere of all the books that a person should read. Many of my own books—*The True Story of the Three Little Pigs*, *The Stinky Cheese Man* (1992), the Time Warp Trio series—are really about other books and stories. I like the idea that one book can point readers to others they might like to read.

In high school, I had a gangly old math teacher—an amazing man—who could sit at his desk facing the class while at the same time writing complex equations on the blackboard behind him. It was like a party trick. And we all thought, *If he can solve these equations backward, we should at least be able to figure them out the usual way.* He had a great sense of humor about math. He made math never seem dry or dull. In *Math Curse* (1995) and the Time Warp Trio books, I wanted to find ways to goof around with science and math too.

> *I can remember in fourth and fifth grade looking on the library shelves for the place where books by me would be.*

Scieszka in his studio with some of his toys

You must talk to a lot of kids.
What is the strangest question you have ever been asked?

A little guy sitting in the front row at a school I visited asked me where I get my shoes. At first I thought he was probably from another planet or something. Then I realized that from where he was sitting, my shoes were about all he could see of the presentation. So he got sort of curious about them.

Do you have a daily work routine?

I can write anywhere—on the subway, on airplanes, or in the park. I always have a pen with me. I'm always ready! I write later drafts on my computer, but I start out in longhand because I can write faster that way.

The main thing is that I try to make myself write every day, no matter what. Sooner or later I write something worth rewriting! I have a notebook full of ideas. When I want to start a book, I come back to that notebook to see if I can get one of those ideas to take off.

Do you revise your work much?

Yes. I was amazed once, going through some old files, to realize how many reams of paper I had gone through before I finished the first Time Warp books. It was kind of scary! I try to polish my work as much as possible before showing it to my editor, because I've found that if I involve other people too soon, it confuses me. I lose track of what it was I wanted to say.

How do you know when a book is done?

I never do know. That's why publishers' deadlines are great for me. The clock is always ticking! Without deadlines, I'd probably write just one picture book every ten years and people would say, "Hmmm. Must be really tough being a writer!"

What is your advice for children who want to write?

Write! I know that sounds stupid, but that's really it. It's good practice to imitate your favorite writers. All writers do that at first. Eventually, if you keep writing, you find your own voice.

Preliminary outline for
Knights of the Kitchen Table

What do you do when you are not writing?

I play basketball, swim, golf, and go bicycling in the park. I considered playing roller hockey when my son started. But then I thought, *Now that looks like a game I could* really *injure myself in!* I also love to read, listen to music, look at art, goof around New York City with my wife, and play with my kids.

Was there a moment when you realized you were no longer a kid?

I remember when I became ten—the double digits!—thinking that that was a big thing. But you said, "No longer a kid"? No, I haven't hit that one yet.

What is the best part of being a writer?

Being a writer is fun, but it's also torture. The hardest part is sitting down to write on a nice summer day. It becomes fun once I get something going, when like an athlete I know I'm "in the zone." That's when ideas come, and that feels magical. But the best part of writing is finishing a good piece of writing.

A JON SCIESZKA Reader

The Good, the Bad, and the Goofy, illustrated by Lane Smith (Viking, 1992; Puffin, 1993)

Knights of the Kitchen Table, illustrated by Lane Smith (Viking, 1991; Puffin, 1993)

Math Curse, illustrated by Lane Smith (Viking, 1995)

The Not-So-Jolly Roger, illustrated by Lane Smith (Viking, 1991; Puffin, 1993)

Squids Will Be Squids: Fresh Morals, Beastly Fables,

illustrated by Lane Smith (Viking, 1998)

The Stinky Cheese Man and Other Fairly Stupid Tales,

illustrated by Lane Smith (Viking, 1992)

The True Story of the Three Little Pigs, by A. Wolf, As Told to Jon Scieszka,

illustrated by Lane Smith (Viking, 1989; Puffin, 1996)

Tut, Tut, illustrated by Lane Smith (Viking, 1996; Puffin, 1998)

2095, illustrated by Lane Smith (Viking, 1995; Puffin, 1997)

Your Mother Was a Neanderthal, illustrated by Lane Smith (Viking, 1993; Puffin, 1995)

∗

SEYMOUR SIMON

(BORN AUGUST 9, 1931, NEW YORK, NEW YORK)

"I have a very childlike imagination and interests," Seymour Simon once said by way of explaining how he goes about choosing the subjects of his books. "If I'm curious about something . . . I'm sure that kids are going to be curious." Simon, who has published more than two hundred science books for young readers, likes knowing that porcupines do not really shoot their quills at their enemy (he wrote about this in *Animal Fact/Animal Fable*, 1979), and that chewing gum is not bad for your teeth and may actually do some good (see *Body Sense, Body Nonsense*, 1981).

Simon taught science to fifth graders and in junior high before writing his first book, *Animals in Field and Laboratory* (1968). He soon wrote others on subjects as varied as the science of motion, weather, paper airplanes, and his favorite field, astronomy. These early books all had black-and-white illustrations. Simon's work took an exciting turn in the 1980s when, for a variety of reasons, it became possible for him to make use of the spectacular new color photographs of space coming from NASA. Having the chance to share these amazing full-color images with young readers in such books as *Jupiter* and *Saturn* (both 1985) thrilled the author. Images like NASA's had been beyond human reach when Simon was a child. They are the first photographs ever, he says with delight, to "match my own feelings of awe about space."

Seymour, age 6

What kind of boy were you?

Smart—and very scientific! I knew the colors of the rainbow very early, the names of all the planets, and what "escape velocity" was. And I was eager to share this information with everyone. I wore glasses by the time I was in third grade.

I went to the movies every Saturday morning and listened to the radio every Sunday evening. A favorite radio show, *The Shadow*, always began with a creepy voice saying, "Who knows what evil lurks in the hearts of men? THE SHADOW KNOWS!"

I loved baseball and was a Yankees fan initially, then a Giants fan. I probably can *still* name the entire Yankees team from the 1930s and '40s, when Joe DiMaggio was their star player.

Did you play ball as a kid?

The Bronx in those days was like a collection of little villages. The neighborhood kids where I lived all played stickball in the street. We measured our hits in the units of distance between sewers. A two-sewer hitter was considered especially good. I could hit maybe one and a half sewers. That made me neither the best nor the worst.

Did you enjoy reading?

> **I realized how wonderful it is to be a writer: Other people have to shut up and listen to you!**

I had twin sisters who were six years older than me. Among their duties was to read to me and later to take me to the library. From hearing the same books read over and over again at home, I learned to read before I started school. Once I had my own library card, I would walk to the public library, take out the maximum number of books, which was four, and read them all by the time I got home.

By the time I was seven I was reading science fiction magazines, which an older cousin gave to me. Soon after that, I began writing letters to the magazines. I would rate the stories and then end the letter with, "I've got to go now. I can hear the rockets blasting off outside." Really childish things like that. Many of these letters got published. They were my first publications, and I was thrilled.

When did you decide you wanted to be a writer?

I always wanted to write. I wrote my first book, called *Space Monsters*, when I was in the second grade. It was about a trip to a zoo on some distant planet. The zoo had cages with monsters collected from all over the universe. My teacher stapled the book together and had me read it to the class. That's when I realized how wonderful it is to be a writer: Other people have to shut up and listen to you!

What else did you like to do as a kid?

I loved visiting the Bronx Zoo, which we got to by trolley car. In those days you could feed the elephants. We'd buy peanuts from the vending machine: It would be one for the elephants and one for us!

When I was ten or eleven my parents gave me my own camera. I had always wanted to draw but never could, so being able to take pictures was great. Film was very expensive, so I thought carefully about every photograph I took. I photographed nature in the city—grass breaking through concrete steps, trees on a city street. I still love to take pictures. I have a quick mind, and photography slows me down so that I look more closely at things, pay better attention.

In junior high school I joined the Junior Astronomy Club, which had its offices in the basement of the Hayden Planetarium of the American Museum of Natural History, in New York City. I'd go down every Saturday to work on the club's magazine. I eventually became club president. All my friends at that time came from the club. We had passes that let us into the museum after hours. Leading astronomers would speak at our monthly meetings. We took field trips to nearby observatories, and listened to classical music together. We had a great time.

> *Photography slows me down so that I look more closely at things, pay better attention.*

Photograph by Simon from
Spring Across America

Was there a moment when you realized you were no longer a child?

Throughout my childhood, the United States had the same president, Franklin Roosevelt. For a long time, in fact, I thought that "Presidentroosevelt" was a single word. FDR's death, in April 1945, when I was fourteen, followed by the end of World War II, felt like the end of my childhood to me. I can remember being in Times Square when news of the dropping of the atomic bomb on Hiroshima flashed across the Times Tower's news ribbon. Most people had never heard of the atomic bomb. But I knew just what kind of a bomb it was because I'd read about such things in my science fiction magazines.

How did you go about becoming a writer?

Before I wrote my first book, I taught junior high school science for many years in Queens. While still teaching I began writing a monthly science column for a fifth-grade magazine called *Scholastic NewsTime*. Finally, I got an idea for a book on animal behavior, sent off a proposal to a publisher, and had it accepted. This was in 1968, when I was thirty-seven. I received great reviews. After that, publishers began to call me.

Photograph of Moon's view of Earth from *Our Solar System*

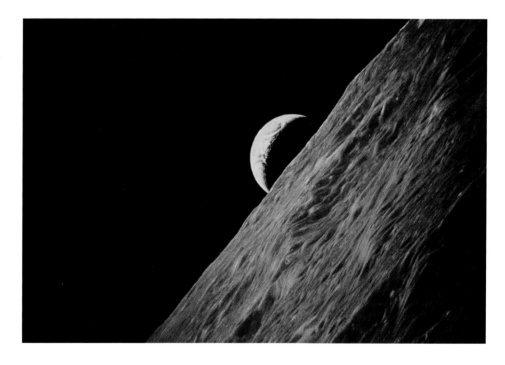

Do you have a daily work routine?

I work in spurts. On days when I'm writing, I'll write until lunch, then I might do some related work like answering mail.

How do you go about making one of your books?

I'll have a subject in mind, discuss it with my editor, then start to do photo research. I have found many of the photos for my space books at NASA in Washington, D.C., or at the Jet Propulsion Laboratory in

California. In the last few years I've also been able to download photos directly from the World Wide Web. Whenever I can, I take my own photographs and do my own field research. For *Whales* (1989), for instance, I went out on a number of whale-watching trips.

I might start with a thousand or more photographs for one of my picture books, then narrow the selection down to two hundred possibilities. Then when I write the book, I get those two hundred down to the final twenty-five.

Tell me about this photograph (at left) from **Our Solar System** *(1992).*
When you look at it, what do you see and think about?

This photo of a crescent Earth over the barren landscape of the Moon was taken by the *Apollo 17* astronauts in 1972. It is still one of my favorite photographs. I think of how lucky we are to be on Earth, a watery, cloud-covered planet, filled with living things. All the other planets and moons in our solar system are harsh, barren places, inhospitable to life. The sight of the blue orb of Earth makes me wonder if there are other planets circling far-distant stars that might support life. And I begin to wonder what they might be like and if I will ever see them.

Do you revise your work?

I usually write about twenty-five percent too much. Revision for me is often a question of cutting, which I do with my editor's help.

How do you know when a book is done?

Beginning for me is always much harder than ending. The further I get into the writing of a book the more involved I become with the material, and the easier it becomes. When I finish, I often have a feeling of exhilaration. I think, *That came out a lot better than I thought it would!*

What do you like to do when you are not writing?

Take pictures. Play with computers—I'm a techno-freak! Take care of my pets. I have two cats and at one time I had nineteen tanks of tropical fish. I've also kept snakes, crickets, spiders, praying mantises, and ants. I was one of the first teachers in the United States to keep gerbils

Simon at his desk with his cat
Sir Isaac Newton

in a classroom. They bred so rapidly that I had to keep giving them away to the kids in my class. I think I populated the Borough of Queens with gerbils!

What do you tell kids who want to write?
That if you're going to become a writer, you have to be a reader first. And that a good way to start writing is by emulating your favorite author. It's only with time that you develop your own voice.

What is the best part of being a writer?
I love finding out everything I can about a subject such as gorillas or hurricanes or black holes in space. For me, the best part of writing science books is doing the research on these fascinating subjects.

A SEYMOUR SIMON Reader

Animal Fact/Animal Fable (Crown, 1979; Crown, 1988)

Animals in Field and Laboratory: Projects in Animal Behavior,
illustrated by Emily Arnold McCully (McGraw-Hill, 1968)

Body Sense, Body Nonsense (Harper, 1981)

Einstein Anderson, Science Detective series, illustrated by Fred Winkowski
(Viking, 1980-) / reillustrated by S. D. Schindler (Morrow, 1997- ; Avon. 1998-)

The Heart (Morrow, 1996; Mulberry, 1999)

Jupiter (Morrow, 1985; Mulberry, 1988)

Our Solar System (Morrow, 1992)

The Paper Airplane Book, illustrated by Byron Barton (Viking, 1971; Puffin, 1976)

Saturn (Morrow, 1985; Mulberry, 1988)

Spring Across America (Hyperion, 1996)

Star Walk (Morrow, 1995)

Whales (Harper, 1989; Harper, 1992)

✳

LAURENCE YEP

(BORN JUNE 14, 1948, SAN FRANCISCO, CALIFORNIA)

"Your first home," Laurence Yep wrote in his autobiography, *The Lost Garden* (1991), "will always be the one that you remember best. I have been away from it for over twenty years; and yet I still go back in my dreams." For Yep, whose father and maternal grandparents emigrated from China, that home was an apartment, and the family grocery store it came with, in an African-American neighborhood of San Francisco. As young people, both he and his older brother, Thomas, helped out at the store. It was there that young Laurence taught himself to juggle while unpacking endless cartons of soup cans. And it was there that he learned about patience, hard work, and getting along with neighbors.

A high school English teacher who set high goals for his students was the first person to encourage Yep to write. The experience of that class changed the direction of his life. Yep was eighteen when he published his first short story, a sci-fi fantasy. He has since written many books and many kinds of books, including picture books, mysteries, historical novels, science fic-tion, fantasy, and realistic stories set in the present day. He has retold Chinese folk stories and written for the theater. In nearly all these varied works, Yep, who is married to the children's book author Joanne Ryder, has returned to questions he has been asking himself since childhood: What does it mean to be Chinese *and* American? What is it like to live the life of an outsider in an alien world or culture? Can one who belongs to two cultures ever feel at home anywhere?

What kind of child were you?

Larry, age 5, in football outfit

Working in our family store, and getting to know our customers, I learned early on how to observe and listen to people, how to relate to others. It was good training for a writer.

Back then, however, I thought of myself as a scientist. I was going to be a chemist. Like my father, I was fascinated by machines. My father wanted to know how machines worked—televisions, for instance. At one time he filled our apartment with old TVs! I, on the other hand, was always asking "What if?" questions about machines. What if the world had a central energy source that broadcast power? There could be world peace because it would be possible to cut off the power to any nation that wanted to start a war.

I was an *American* child—so relentlessly so that my grandmother became hesitant to talk about Chinese things with me, even about the gods she kept on her bedroom bureau. I regretted this later, when I wanted to know more about my Chinese heritage.

Did you enjoy reading?

Both my parents were good readers, and I became one too. The Oz books were among my favorite books. Fantasy led to science fiction. When it came to realistic stories, however, I found nothing as a kid about the lives of Chinese-Americans. I know now that there was nothing for adults to read, either.

Were there good storytellers in your family?

All my relatives were good storytellers. My auntie Mary was probably the best. She would tell scary family stories, including some about West Virginia, where she and my mother and their brother grew up. There was the story, for instance, about Aunt Mary and my mother as girls taking a shortcut to school through a farmer's field. They were chronically late for school, in part because my mother was so slow to get dressed, and because all girls in those days—the 1920s—wore many layers of clothing, especially in winter. Every morning the principal would play a record over the school intercom. The music could be heard all around. When the music stopped, it meant you were late for school and would be punished!

So here were my mother and Aunt Mary walking up the hill. They could hear the music floating down. Knowing they didn't have very long, they cut across the field, stepping high through waist-high snow. All of a sudden, they heard a snorting sound behind them. They turned and saw a little steam cloud. The steam cloud was coming closer and closer. They realized it was a bull! The bull was coming after them. The high snow meant that they could not run away. The high snow also meant that the bull couldn't move any faster than they could. It was all like a movie with everything happening in slow motion and music playing in the background!

When did you first think of yourself as a storyteller, as a writer?

As a child, I never thought of myself as the storyteller of the family, because the others were always better at it than I was. I got interested in writing purely by chance, thanks to a high school English teacher, the Reverend John Becker. He challenged us not to set limits for ourselves. He told us all to write a story or poem that would be published in a national magazine. That's when I began writing science fiction, which I found was a lot like doing a lab experiment. I could set up a society, give it inhabitants, decide on certain parameters or rules, and then ask myself what might happen next.

What was your first story about?

It was about a time when San Francisco had sunk underneath the ocean. A young man goes back to the underwater ruins, trying to discover his roots. Finally, he decides that the only thing he can know about himself is that he's human. The irony is that he's *not* human, but a genetically altered dolphin. The reader knows this, but he never finds out.

Years later I realized that all my science fiction stories, including that first one, were about alien creatures—or about alienated heroes. And I realized that in writing those stories I was really trying to work my way through to a clearer sense of who I was as a Chinese-American.

Yep (second from right) with cast of the 1992 Kennedy Center production of *Dragonwings*, adapted from the author's novel

How has being of Chinese heritage been important to you?

The answer to that question has changed dramatically more than once. As a child I hated Chinese school. I wanted to be as American as possible. Then, in my early twenties, I became very interested in my Chinese roots.

For years after that, I thought that my function as a Chinese-American writer was to act as a bridge between two cultures. Now, though, I am not so sure that it is possible to blend two cultures together. Asian cultures are family- and cooperation-oriented. American culture on the other hand emphasizes the individual and competition. The two cultures pull in opposite directions. So I see myself now as someone who will always be on the border between two cultures. That works to my benefit as a writer because not quite fitting in helps me be a better observer.

> **Not quite fitting in helps me be a better observer.**

Do you have a daily work routine?

I have always tried to have a separate area in which to work. When I started out, it was the corner of a room. Now I have my own study. I have also always tried to write at the same time each day. There's a reason for this. Writing is raising a window so that other people can look inside your world and your imagination. If you have a set place and a set time, sometimes that window will start rising on its own.

Paying attention to your senses is the first step toward being creative. Before I begin work, I'll do breathing exercises during which I close my eyes. It's a kind of trick. Humans are primarily visual creatures, and when we close our eyes the brain becomes starved for visual information. When I finally open up my eyes, I get a flood of visual information and feel I've reconnected myself with the world and am ready to begin.

What kinds of research do you do for your books?

Old newspapers are like time machines for me, even down to the advertisements. In college, while doing an independent study on Chinese-American history, I came across two old articles about the turn-of-the-century Chinese-American aviator upon whose story I later based *Dragonwings* (1975). I also like to read old maps and study old photographs. From sources such as these, I've learned, for instance, that in San Francisco's Chinatown in the late 1800s there were three shooting galleries and some lumberyards. If you were walking through the streets in those days, you might have heard the pop pop pop of shooting gallery guns going off and the sound of hand-powered saws. I put background noises such as these into my stories because they make for more vivid writing. By now, having done so much research, when I go for a walk in Chinatown I can "see" all the long-gone buildings that lined the streets at different times in the past.

I feel a responsibility as a Chinese-American not to make up facts about the past. Frequently before I begin to tackle a difficult subject about Chinese-Americans, I'll write a science fiction story. I like doing this because I know that if I write about Alpha Centauri, I won't have to worry about my responsibility to the Alpha Centaurians!

Do you revise your work?

I rewrote *Dragon of the Lost Sea* (1982) seven times. It started out as a story about two suburban kids who were taken to a world based on Chinese mythology. But toward the end of the book I introduced two

> *I found nothing as a kid to read about the lives of Chinese Americans. I know now that there was nothing for adults to read, either.*

Manuscript page from
The Amah

Yep/ **Amah 12** (Cinderella Effect)   March 4, 1998   96

said.

"Well, why don't we order a pizza." Stephanie ~~started to unsling her purse.~~ "My treat."

Mama had been cutting up food all day in preparation for a home-cooked Chinese meal. "But Mama—" I began to tell her.

However, Mama cut in quickly. "I would insist on paying. You're our guest."

Stephanie and Mama argued for a little bit—that part reminded me of a Chinese meal anyway where everyone wants to pick up the check—but eventually Stephanie gave in. Of course, the ~~brats~~ *kids* all wanted different toppings on the pizza.

I was going to tell them to order a pizza with everything like we always did but Stephanie suggested, "Why don't we order four?"

I think Mama did a mental gulp over our finances but smiled bravely. "Good idea," she said.

When Stephanie started to set the table, I noticed how quick ~~the brats~~ *my brothers and sisters* jumped to help her. No pouting. No screaming. No pleading. No threats. They were truly under Cinderella's spell.

When the pizza arrived, ~~though,~~ Mama wouldn't allow us to eat it right away. "Wait, wait." She hurried into the kitchen but a moment later I heard her calling to me. "Amy, where's the teapot?"

"On the bottom shelf," I said. I was terribly hungry smelling the pizza, ~~but of course I couldn't eat it."~~

A moment later, Mama shouted. "No, not that one. The *special* teapot."

That gave me a start. Now I knew how much Mama treasured Miss Stephanie. She had never brought the teapot out for my friends.

[handwritten marginalia: Yes, but Chinese can be incredibly forceful to involve face. I've seen my father literally wrestle an uncle.]

[handwritten marginalia: wouldn't her father have insisted she pay?]

minor characters, a dragon and her pet boy, who became such vivid characters for me that I finally realized that the story had to be about them.

Do you ever get stuck and not know what to write next?

Often! I'll feel myself running out of gas. When that happens I know it's time to put that book aside and move on to a different project. Frequently I'll write several books at once but in different genres. I wrote *The Mark Twain Murders* (1982), a murder mystery set in nineteenth-century San Francisco, for example, at the same time that I was working on *Dragon of the Lost Sea*. As different as they are, both those books describe the humorous interaction between a younger character and an older character as they make their way through a violent universe.

How do you know when a book is done?

I don't know, because a book is never really done.

What do you tell children who want to write?

That there are many ways to get into a writing mood. During school visits, I'll ask for a list of objects in the room. We'll choose one object—a lightbulb, say—and try to imagine it as a living creature. How would a lightbulb communicate with others? How would it get its food? We then try to imagine the creature's world. The last step is to make up a story about that world.

What is the best part of being a writer?

It's nice being able to daydream and to get paid for it.

A LAURENCE YEP Reader

The Amah (Putnam, 1999)

Child of the Owl (Harper, 1977; Harper, 1990)

Dragon of the Lost Sea (Harper, 1982; Harper, 1988)

The Dragon Prince: A Beauty and the Beast Tale,
illustrated by Kam Mak (Harper, 1997; Harper, 1999)

Dragonwings (Harper, 1975; Harper, 1977)

Later, Gator (Hyperion, 1995; Hyperion, 1997)

The Lost Garden: A Memoir (Messner, 1991; Beech Tree, 1996)

The Mark Twain Murders (Four Winds, 1982)

The Rainbow People (reteller), illustrated by David Wiesner (Harper, 1989; Harper, 1992)

The Serpent's Children (Harper, 1984; Harper, 1996)

✳

Photo Credits

Page 3: George Cooper ✷ *Page 4:* Book cover for *Are You There God? It's Me, Margaret.*, courtesy of Simon & Schuster ✷ *Page 4:* Courtesy of Judy Blume ✷ *Page 8:* Manuscript page from *Here's to You, Rachel Robinson,* reproduced by permission of Judy Blume and the Kerlan Collection, University of Minnesota ✷ *Page 10:* Courtesy of Bruce Brooks ✷ *Page 11:* Courtesy of Bruce Brooks ✷ *Page 13:* Leonard S. Marcus ✷ *Page 14:* Manuscript page from *Vanishing,* reproduced by permission of Bruce Brooks ✷ *Page 16:* Courtesy of Karen Cushman ✷ *Page 17:* Courtesy of Karen Cushman ✷ *Page 18:* Courtesy of Karen Cushman ✷ *Page 20:* Courtesy of Karen Cushman ✷ *Page 20:* Manuscript page for *The Ballad of Lucy Whipple,* reproduced by permission of Karen Cushman ✷ *Page 22:* Leonard S. Marcus ✷ *Page 23:* Courtesy of Russell Freedman ✷ *Page 25:* Roy Andrews Collection, Special Collections and University Archives, University of Oregon ✷ *Page 26:* Leonard S. Marcus ✷ *Page 27:* Manuscript page from *Children of the West,* reproduced by permission of Russell Freedman ✷ *Page 29:* Courtesy of Lee Bennett Hopkins ✷ *Page 30:* Courtesy of Lee Bennett Hopkins ✷ *Page 30:* Courtesy of Lee Bennett Hopkins; copyright © 1977 by Alfred A. Knopf, Inc. Used by permission of Alfred A. Knopf, a division of Random House, Inc. ✷ *Pages 32-33:* "When I Dance" by Lee Bennett Hopkins. Copyright © 1997 by Lee Bennett Hopkins. Appears in *Song and Dance,* published by Simon & Schuster Books for Young Readers. Reprinted by permission of Curtis Brown, Ltd. ✷ *Page 35:* Betsy Imershein ✷ *Page 36:* Courtesy of James Howe ✷ *Page 39:* Elena Blanco ✷ *Page 39:* Jane Collins ✷ *Page 40:* Notes for *Bunnicula,* reproduced by permission of James Howe ✷ *Page 42:* David Kaplan; courtesy of Johanna Hurwitz ✷ *Page 43:* Courtesy of Johanna Hurwitz ✷ *Page 46:* Manuscript page from *The Llama in the Library,* reproduced by permission of Johanna Hurwitz ✷ *Page 47:* Courtesy of Johanna Hurwitz ✷ *Page 49:* Courtesy of E.L. Konigsburg ✷ *Page 50:* Courtesy of E.L. Konigsburg ✷ *Page 53:* Reprinted with the permission of Atheneum Books for Young Readers, an imprint of Simon & Schuster Children's Publishing Division from a July 21, 1966 letter from Jean Karl to E. L. Konigsburg accepting the manuscript for *From the Mixed-up Files of Mrs. Basil E. Frankweiler* ✷ *Page 55:* Photo courtesy of E. L Konigsburg and the University of Pittsburgh ✷ *Page 55:* Illustration by E. L. Konigsburg; courtesy of the University of Pittsburgh. Reprinted with permission of Atheneum Books for Young Readers, an imprint of Simon & Schuster Children's Publishing Division from *From the Mixed-up Files of Mrs. Basil E. Frankweiler,* written and illustrated by E. L. Konigsburg. Copyright © 1967 E. L. Konigsburg. ✷ *Page 58:* Courtesy of Lois Lowry ✷ *Page 59:* Courtesy of Lois Lowry ✷ *Page 60:* Courtesy of Lois Lowry ✷ *Page 63:* Courtesy of Lois Lowry ✷ *Page 64:* Susan Richman; by permission of Scholastic Inc. ✷ *Page 65:* Courtesy of Ann M. Martin ✷ *Page 67:* Courtesy of Ann M. Martin ✷ *Page 70:* Leonard S. Marcus ✷ *Page 71:* Courtesy of Nicholasa Mohr ✷ *Page 73:* Illustration from *Nilda,* reproduced by permission of Nicholasa Mohr ✷ *Page 74:* Tom Brazil; courtesy of Henry Street Settlement ✷ *Page 76:* Ruth Wright Paulsen ✷ *Page 77:* Courtesy of Gary Paulsen ✷ *Page 78:* Rick Schrock ✷ *Page 80:* Courtesy of Gary Paulsen ✷ *Page 83:* Brian Smale; by permission of Penguin Putnam ✷ *Page 84:* Courtesy of Jon Scieszka ✷ *Page 86:* Casey Scieszka ✷ *Page 88:* Notes for *Knights of the Kitchen Table,* reproduced by permission of Jon Scieszka ✷ *Page 90:* Courtesy of Seymour Simon ✷ *Page 91:* Courtesy of Seymour Simon ✷ *Page 93:* Photograph from *Spring Across America,* reproduced by permission of Seymour Simon ✷ *Page 94:* NASA photograph; courtesy of Seymour Simon ✷ *Page 96:* Leonard S. Marcus ✷ *Page 97:* Courtesy of Laurence Yep ✷ *Page 98:* Courtesy of Laurence Yep ✷ *Page 100:* Courtesy of Laurence Yep ✷ *Page 102:* Manuscript page for *The Amah,* reproduced by permission of Laurence Yep